D0491752

# LOAVES AND FISHES

an illustrated history of the

Ministry of Agriculture, Fisheries and Food

1889 - 1989

by
Susan Foreman

LONDON: HER MAJESTY'S STATIONERY OFFICE

© Crown copyright 1989

First published 1989

ISBN 0 11 242823 1

HMSO publications are available from:

**HMSO Publications Centre**
(Mail and telephone orders only)
PO Box 276, London, SW8 5DT
Telephone orders 01-873 9090
General enquiries 01-873 0011
(queuing system in operation for both numbers)

**HMSO Bookshops**
49 High Holborn, London, WC1V 6HB    01-873 0011 (Counter service only)
258 Broad Street, Birmingham, B1 2HE    021-643 3740
Southey House, 33 Wine Street, Bristol, BS1 2BQ    (0272) 264306
9–21 Princess Street, Manchester, M60 8AS    061-834 7201
80 Chichester Street, Belfast, BT1 4JY    (0232) 238451
71 Lothian Road, Edinburgh, EH3 9AZ    031-228 4181

**HMSO's Accredited Agents**
(see Yellow Pages)

*and through good booksellers*

Printed in the United Kingdom for Her Majesty's Stationery Office
Dd. 290759  C60  3/89

# CONTENTS

# ACKNOWLEDGEMENTS

Many have contributed to my research for this book, and it is my pleasure to acknowledge here their assistance and expertise. I made the greatest demands on the Library and the Photographic Unit of the Ministry of Agriculture, Fisheries and Food, without whom much fascinating material would have eluded me, and they deserve to be mentioned first. However, many varied parts of MAFF also made valuable contributions, and I should particularly like to thank the staff of the Directorate of Fisheries Research at Lowestoft, the staff of the *MAFF Bulletin*, the Publicity branch and Record Review section at Chessington, and Paul Bartlett and Douglas d'Enno for their help and interest.

I also received many kindnesses from the staff of the Royal Botanic Gardens, Kew, the Institute of Agricultural History and Museum of English Rural Life at Reading, and the archivist of the Library of the University of Reading. I am grateful for help received from the BBC Written Archive Centre at Caversham, the History of Advertising Trust, the National Stud, the Public Record Office (sources cited as INF and MAF), and the National Portrait Gallery archive. The libraries of other Whitehall Departments also supplied much valued assistance, and I am particularly indebted to those at the Foreign and Commonwealth Office and the Department of Trade and Industry. The London Library was, as always, a splendid and unique source of material, as were the Departments of Art and Photographs and the Library at the Imperial War Museum.

Finally I owe a special thank you to staff in the Graphic Design Unit and Publications Department at HMSO for their sympathetic designs and attention to detail in my book.

To all these, and many others, my thanks.

Susan Foreman
Rickmansworth
October 1988

# PICTURE SOURCES

*Walter Runciman, President of the Board of Agriculture and Fisheries, 1911–1914*

*Earl of Selborne, President of the Board of Agriculture and Fisheries, 1915–1916*

*Lord Lee of Fareham, Minister of Agriculture and Fisheries, 1920–1921*

*W S Morrison, Minister of Food, 1939–1940*

*1. Past Presidents and Ministers*

*Colonel J J Llewellin, Minister of Food, 1943–1945*

*Christopher Soames, Minister of Agriculture, Fisheries and Food, 1960–1964*

*T F Peart, Minister of Agriculture, Fisheries and Food, 1964–1968 and 1974–1976*

*Cledwyn Hughes, Minister of Agriculture, Fisheries and Food, 1968–1970*

The Ministry of Ag. and Fish
Does everything that one could wish
To foster, guide and chaperon
Those industries it calls its own;
And it would be unkind to chaff
The members of its faithful staff
Who seek no rest and find no peace,
But labour always to increase,
By deeds of department derring,
Corn, flesh and fowl and good red herring.

No slackness is allowed to smirch
Their splendid record of research,
No doubts molest their firm reliance
On methods blessed by modern science.
One expert in his spacious lab.,
Observes the habits of the crab;
Another takes his grain of wheat,
His whiting or his sugar beet
And tries by some ingenious test
What mode of living suits it best;
While others dedicate their lives
To proving how the ploughman thrives
Who mitigates his dull vocation
With intellectual recreation,
And spends an hour of leisure daily
Playing upon the ukelele.

The farmer strolling round his paddock,
The fisherman in quest of haddock,
Unite to sing with grateful glee
The praises of their Ministry.
Rude simple souls, they lack that store
Of expert scientific lore
On which alone success depends,
And this their kind Department sends.
For, if calamities befall
The men who till, the men who trawl –
If beasts contract the foot-and-mouth,
If blizzards blow from north or south,
If prices slump and credit fails,
If nets are rent by sportive whales,
The Staff is ready in a trice
To help them with its best advice,
On land or sea, in drought or storm,
Sent free of charge in pamphlet form.

CLM, in *Punch*, 20 April, 1927

2. The main entrance of the Ministry of Agriculture, Fisheries and Food, Whitehall Place, London SW1

ix

# PROLOGUE

*IN THE GREATEST PART OF THESE KINGDOMS, THE PRINCIPLES OF AGRICULTURE ARE NOT YET SUFFICIENTLY UNDERSTOOD, NOR ARE THE IMPLEMENTS OF HUSBANDRY, OR THE STOCK OF THE FARMER, BROUGHT TO THAT PERFECTION OF WHICH THEY ARE CAPABLE.*

Sir J Sinclair. *Address to the House of Commons*, 1793

*3. Presidents of the first Board of Agriculture*

The Board of Agriculture, now MAFF, was established in 1889. Its establishment had been pioneered by a distinguished predecessor, also named the Board of Agriculture, which was in being from 1793 to 1822. Founded by Royal Charter on 23rd August 1793 as the Board or Society for the Encouragement of Agriculture and Internal Improvement, the first Board was given a grant-in-aid of £3,000 a year. That eminent agricultural amateur, Arthur Young, had wagered a set of his *Annals of Agriculture* against a set of the *Statistical Accounts of Scotland* (compiled in 21 volumes) by Sir John Sinclair that it would never happen. 'Your Board of Agriculture will be in the moon' he remarked to Sir John, but added percipiently, 'if on earth, remember I am to be Secretary'.

Sir John had long petitioned the Prime Minister for such an organisation, and having earned Pitt's gratitude through services in connection with a little matter of an issue of Exchequer Bills, the first Board of Agriculture was finally established in 1793. It was constituted (like the Board of Trade) of numerous ex-officio members, including the Archbishops of Canterbury and York, the Lord Chancellor, the Lord President of the Council, the Speaker, the President of the Royal Society, Master General of the Ordnance, and the Surveyor-General of Woods and Forests, plus 30 ordinary members. The President was Sir John Sinclair and Arthur Young was appointed Secretary. He was not very happy with his salary of £400 a year, especially as strict attendance was expected and all, including the clerks, worked in a room in Sinclair's house.

Great stress was laid on the importance of instituting an agricultural survey of every county and inquiring into means of improvement of the land. This proved over-

1

ambitious with the comparatively small funds available, and the result was the 'production of a huge mass of ill-digested articles of the most varying degrees of merit . . . and the issue [they were entered at Stationers' Hall] of such unreliable literature brought the Board at once into bad repute'. The Board also published 'communications' on various agricultural subjects and extracts from prize essays, and originated and pushed through Parliament several useful agricultural measures.

Growing discontent with Sir John Sinclair's somewhat high-handed methods led to his being voted out of office in favour of Lord Somerville in 1798, and to new premises at 32 Sackville Street. Under Somerville, the Board's financial position was improved, an experimental farm proposed, and annual prizes awarded for the best essays on given agricultural subjects. He was followed by Lord Carrington in 1800, during whose tenure great efforts were made to bring about the general enclosure and cultivation of the country's waste lands as a panacea for the then depressed state of British agriculture, and as a means of making Britain independent of foreign supplies. The Board's first general enclosure bill prepared in 1798 was thrown out by the Lords, their second in 1801 was also opposed and the Board itself attacked by the House.

Sir John Sinclair was again elected President in 1806, much to the annoyance of Arthur Young, who noted in his diary: 'Nothing but bad news. Sir J Banks writes me that J Sinclair is to resume the chair of the Board under promises of good behaviour.' Sinclair's second term was mainly devoted to his project of completing the agricultural surveys in their corrected form. He retired from the Presidency in 1813, but continued attending as an ordinary member.

With the publication of the last agricultural surveys, the Board was at a loss as to how to spend its annual Parliamentary grant of £3,000, apart from the offer of annual premiums. It therefore decided to apply for only £1,000 for the year 1819. As Ernest Clarke, writing in the *Journal of the Royal Agricultural Society of England* in 1898 said: 'A step of greater inanity could hardly have been taken'. The Treasury promptly seized the opportunity of saving the grant and, after the death of Arthur Young in 1820, a letter from the Treasury office dated 24th October 1820 intimated that 'the Lords of His Majesty's Treasury did not feel themselves justified in recommending to

Parliament to make any further grant for the service of the Board of Agriculture.'

The Board was then on its own, and efforts were made to maintain it under its existing charter by members' donations and subscriptions. Petitions were several times unsuccessfully presented to the Treasury for some financial support, and on a review of the financial position in May 1822 it was found that the subscriptions received were inadequate. The Board was dissolved and the Sackville Street premises disposed of. Records and other documents were sent to the Record Office in the Tower of London and the balance of funds of £519.14s.2d. transmitted to the Chancellor of the Exchequer. The Board's final meeting was held on 25th June 1822.

However, its work was not forgotten and many of its functions were taken over by the Royal Agricultural Society of England. The Society was founded in 1838 and held its first show in 1839, its objective being the general advancement of English agriculture. Two other projects proposed by the Board – the compulsory commutation of tithes and the passing of a general enclosure act were adopted about the same time.

Other significant predecessors of the second Board of Agriculture (now MAFF) were the Tithe Commission and the Cattle Plague Department. The Tithe Commission had been set up in 1841 under a provision of the 1836 Tithe Act, with the duty of commuting the tithes into cash payments based on the current corn yield of the land and the average price of corn over a seven-year period. By the Settled Land Act 1882, the Enclosure Commissioners, the Copyhold Commissioners and the Tithe Commissioners were amalgamated under the title of the Land Commissioners for England and Wales, responsible to the Home Secretary. They were transferred to the new Board of Agriculture as its Land Department in 1889.

The Cattle Plague Department was brought into being by the Home Office to combat a virulent virus disease, also known as rinderpest, that broke out in London in June 1865 and spread rapidly over the country. The following year the Department became the Veterinary Department of the Privy Council, and an official Veterinary Service has functioned continuously and effectively ever since. The Veterinary Department went on to administer a series of acts for control of animal diseases and insect pests. In 1883 it took over responsibility for the publication of annual

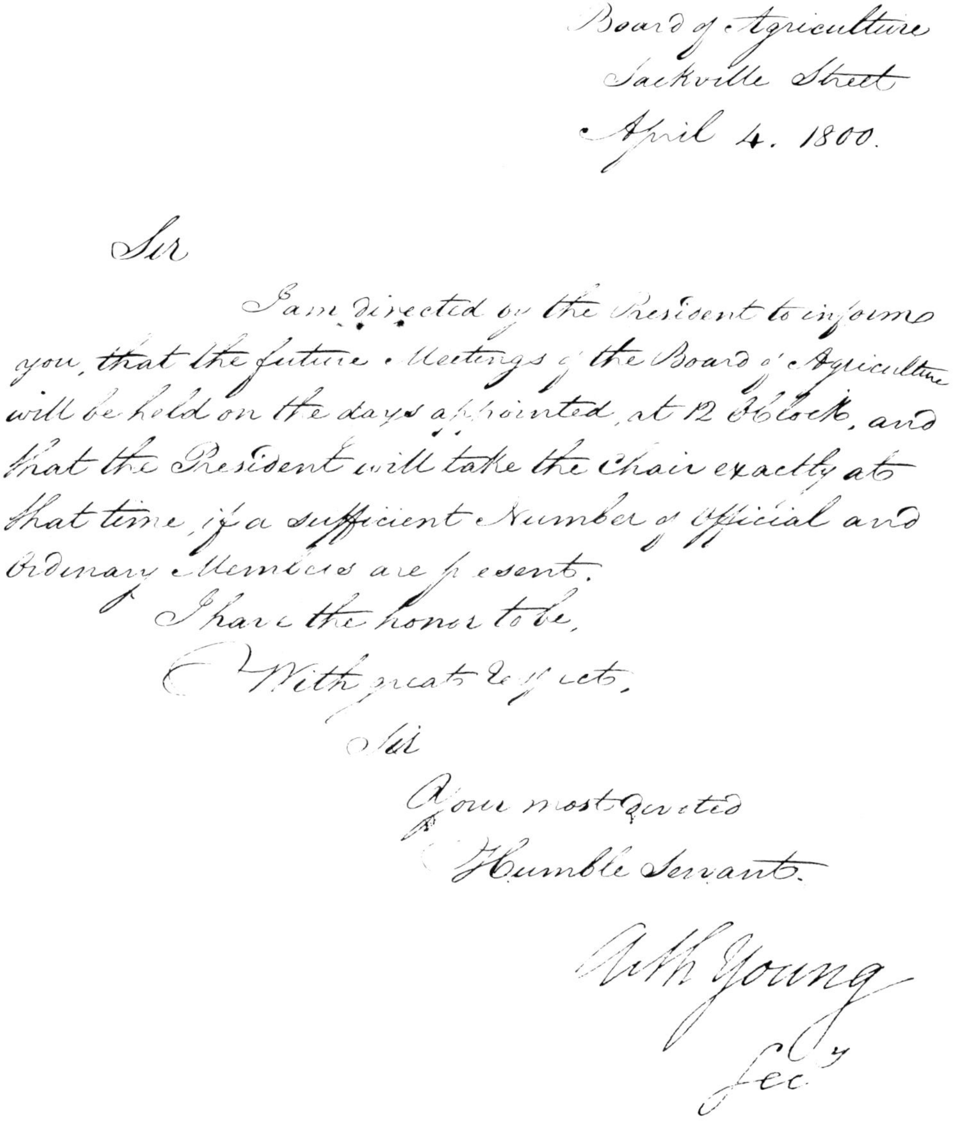

Board of Agriculture
Sackville Street
April 4. 1800.

Sir

I am directed by the President to inform you, that the future Meetings of the Board of Agriculture will be held on the days appointed, at 12 OClock, and that the President will take the Chair exactly at that time, if a sufficient Number of Official and Ordinary Members are present.

I have the honor to be,

With great Respects,

Sir

Your most devoted

Humble Servant.

Arth Young
Sec.

*4. Letter from Arthur Young,*
*Secretary to the first Board of*
*Agriculture, in his own hand*

agricultural statistics from the Board of Trade, although collection of these remained with the Inland Revenue Department. The Veterinary Department was transferred to the Board of Agriculture in 1889.

These were difficult times for farmers. The 'great depression' in agriculture was ascribed to a change in the general level of prices, the growth of free trade in the middle of the 19th century, and the influence of the Industrial Revolution by which agriculture lost its position as the primary source of the nation's wealth and the livelihood of many of its people. Imports of low-priced corn and meat led to a severe fall in prices, and a run of bad harvests in the 1870s reduced output and increased costs. Successive outbreaks of pleuropneumonia and foot-and-mouth disease added to farmers' troubles, and there were further falls in prices for meat, livestock and dairy products. Farmers began to cut back on repairs and maintenance of buildings and fields. The Royal Commission on Agriculture reported in 1882: 'There prevails complete uniformity of conviction as to the great extent and intensity of the distress which has fallen upon the agricultural community ... all without distinction have been involved in a general calamity.'

The Government was frequently asked to bring all its functions relating to agriculture under one Minister, and in 1883 a Committee of the Privy Council for consideration of all matters relating to agriculture was set up. This did not satisfy the agricultural representatives in Parliament, and a Bill was introduced unsuccessfully in 1888 for the establishment of a Board of Agriculture. It surfaced again in 1889 and was finally passed on 12th August.

There was ample debate beforehand, Mr W H Smith (First Lord of the Treasury), moving the second reading on 3rd June 1889, saying that there had for some time been a strong wish for a department responsible for the interests of agriculture, a feeling increased by the depression that had existed in the industry for the last few years – not confined to the propertied classes, but felt by agricultural labourers too. In many parts of the country land had been allowed to go out of cultivation ... 'We cannot hope to teach farmers their business or to improve prices or production, but we might do good by organisation and direction.'

There was some discussion about the form the new body should take – Mr Heneage MP declared that an almost unanimous desire was expressed for a Minister of Agriculture rather than a Board; 'The First Lord has said the Board of Agriculture is to be similar in constitution to the Board of Trade and the Local Government Board; ... I must point out that these Boards have never been called together for consultative purposes, and that to all practical intents they have been absolutely useless ... My desire is that there shall be a responsible Minister, that he shall be accessible to deputations and to all who wish to see and consult him, and that when he has stated his opinion and made an answer to a deputation that answer shall be carried out.'

The first president of the new Board was the Rt. Hon. Henry Chaplin, of whom the *Mark Lane Express* said approvingly, 'In Mr Chaplin are combined the materials which constitute a discreet statesman and a thoroughly well-tried agriculturalist.'

# PART I

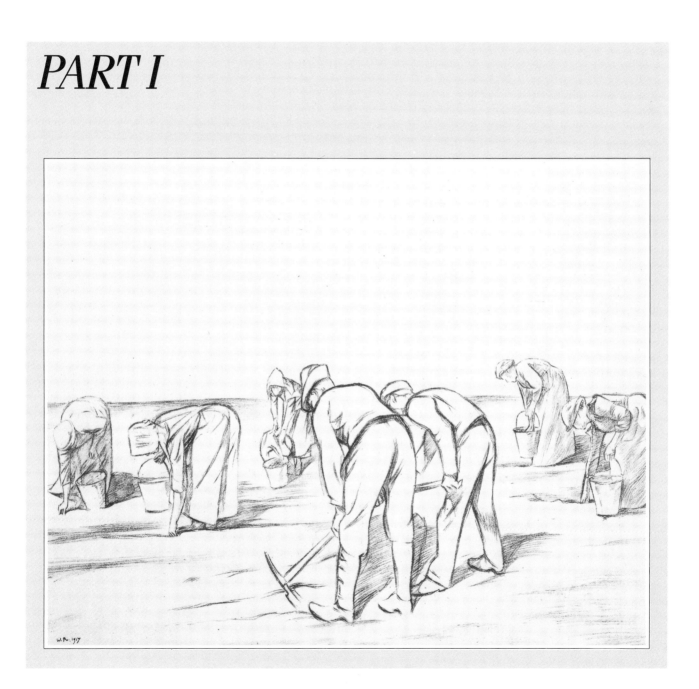

# 1 THE BOARD OF AGRICULTURE 1889-1914

*ONE GOVERNMENT DEPARTMENT... HAS A HISTORY UNLIKE THAT OF ANY OF THE OTHERS – THE BOARD OF AGRICULTURE.*

Gretton, R H. *The King's government*, G Bell, 1913

The Board of Agriculture was established by the 1889 Board of Agriculture Act, and all the functions relating to agriculture were combined under one man, with Mr Chaplin appointed President at a salary of £2,000 a year by Lord Salisbury. The new Board took over the powers and duties of the Land Commissioners and those of the Privy Council under the Contagious Diseases (Animals) acts and the Destructive Insects Act 1877, responsibility for the Ordnance Survey, for the collection and preparation of statistics, and for agricultural research and education.

Membership was composed, in a way similar to the Board of Trade a century earlier, of high officers of state such as the Lord President of the Council, the Chancellor of the Exchequer, and the principal Secretaries of State. But the Board never met, and its powers were exercised by the President or, in emergency, by any member of the Board. The staff numbered 90 and the first annual estimate was for £55,000, of which £5,000 was intended as a grant towards agricultural and dairy schools.

In 1903 an Order in Council gave responsibility to the Board for the Royal Botanic Gardens at Kew, and in the same year an Act was passed to transfer to the newly-styled Board of Agriculture and Fisheries certain powers and duties relating to the fishing industry. The Board had already been authorised to conduct experiments and research, and to promote the agricultural industry, while the Board of Trade remained in charge of surveying and registering vessels, granting certificates to masters and mates, signing on crews, and for discipline, welfare, wrecks and casualties. Most of the Fisheries division work was devoted to the scientific investigation of problems, especially as directed by the International Council for the Exploration of the Sea, which is still in being today. These

*5. Henry Chaplin, appointed first President of the Board of Agriculture, 1889*

investigations were mainly concerned with the increase and preservation of the stock against exploitation. In 1903 the Board of Agriculture also became responsible for the appointment of Fisheries Inspectors and under the Salmon & Freshwater Fisheries Act 1907 it was empowered to constitute and regulate fishery boards and districts by means of provisional orders which also permitted the fishery boards to charge licence duties for freshwater fish.

A separate Board of Agriculture for Scotland was set up in 1911 and took over all the duties relating to Scotland except in the area of animal health. An equivalent Department for Northern Ireland was established in 1921, and since 1978 the Secretary of State for Wales has been responsible for Welsh agricultural affairs.

1903 also saw the launch of the Imperial Preference Campaign by Joseph Chamberlain, a past President of the Board of Trade (1880–85). A number of Conservatives and Liberals were among his supporters and were later to play a significant part in developing Britain's food policies in the first world war. They included Lords Selborne and Milner, and Henry Chaplin, first President of the Board of Agriculture. In 1903 a Committee of the Tariff Commission investigated British agriculture and reported on the country's growing dependence on imported foodstuffs at a time when other countries were becoming self-sufficient in food. 'There is no risk of a total cessation of our supplies . . . no reasonable probability of serious interference with them, and . . . even during a maritime war, there will be no material diminution in their volume', declared the Commissioners with some complacency. So a *laissez-faire* policy for agriculture was allowed to continue, although much land was only half farmed, thousands of tenants were made bankrupt, and the rural population dwindled as workers flocked to the towns, or emigrated to seek work. The import of foreign foodstuffs had become a flood.

In 1904 the Board appointed honorary agricultural correspondents in all parts of the country to keep it in touch with any special circumstances affecting agriculture, horticulture or forestry, and to give advice to farmers. 'I want farmers all over the country to feel that there is someone they can go to and that that someone is in touch with the central office in London; that all this scientific and technical knowledge we have is there only to be placed at the disposal of the farmers', said the President, the Earl of Onslow. 'It is most desirable . . . to do everything we can to

7. *Sir Thomas Elliott, Permanent Secretary, consulting the President, Lord Onslow, 1904*

LORD ROSEBERY at Sheffield: "There are those who, like Mr. Chamberlain, went the whole hog, and might be expressly denoted by the title of whole hoggers."

8. *Joseph Chamberlain launched the Imperial Preference Campaign in 1903*

keep the small tenant farmers, and even the small owners in the country upon their farms, and I believe a great deal . . . may be done by showing them that they really have a friend in the Board of Agriculture.'

The total agricultural area of Great Britain declined only slightly between 1875 and 1914, but the whole nature of farming changed during that period. The area under crops other than grass fell by about 4,400,000 acres, and the numbers of sheep had dropped, whereas the numbers of dairy and beef cattle, pigs and poultry, had increased. Workers employed in agriculture had gone down from 2,800,000 in 1871 to 2,200,000 in 1911. The increase in low cost imports and consequent low prices led to this decline.

By 1914, despite Lord Lucas seeing 'no occasion whatever for public alarm over food supplies', the output of home-grown food met only about one-third of the country's annual needs. No serious effort had been made to increase British farms' output before the war and Government intervention was limited to the encouragement of scientific research and enforcement of the laws against the adulteration of food. As late as October 1916, Walter Runciman, then President of the Board of Trade was saying in the House that 'the thing that we ought to avoid in this country is . . . to put ourselves in the position of a blockaded people . . . we want to avoid any rationing of our people in food.'

So the outbreak of war did not immediately lead to any significant changes in the work or organisation of the Board of Agriculture and Fisheries.

*9. Contemporary postcards*

*10. Liberal Party campaign poster, January 1906*

# 2 WORLD WAR ONE
## AGRICULTURE

*GIVE THE FARMERS AS MUCH LABOUR AS THEY CAN USE. COMPEL THEM TO PLANT THE CROP THAT THE GOVERNMENT THINK MOST ESSENTIAL. COMPEL THEM TO PRODUCE FOOD, AND COMMANDEER THE FOOD WHEN IT IS PRODUCED AT A FAIR PRICE TO THE FARMERS.*

Mr G Lambert, speaking on the *New Ministries and Secretaries Bill,* 20th December 1916

During the first two years of war people did not want for food because there were bumper harvests and little interruption to food imports. The Board was well aware of the importance of ensuring that enough skilled men should be retained on the land to keep it in cultivation, and an inquiry was carried out in August 1914 as to how mobilisation would affect labour for that year's harvest. The indiscriminate manner of recruitment together with better wages had allowed some of the best farmworkers – horsemen, stockmen, shepherds – to join up. The Board, in co-operation with the Board of Trade, recommended that farmers should make full use of their local Labour Exchanges, encouraged them to use female labour, and in June 1915 arranged with the Army Council that furlough should be given to a limited number of men to work on the harvest and that skilled men should not, for the time being, be recruited.

In 1915 Asquith appointed the Earl of Selborne as President of the Board of Agriculture, and a Committee chaired by Lord Milner, with Rowland Prothero as one of its members, was set up in June that year to consider the need for action to maintain and increase food production in England and Wales – assuming that the war went on beyond September 1916. 'A set of men more absolutely divided, not only on first principles, but in their appreciation of the facts with which they had to deal were never seated round one table', said Milner. The Committee's recommendations for a guaranteed price for wheat and for District Committees to be set up by each county were rejected.

However, Lord Selborne did succeed in creating the County War Agricultural Committees, made up of local landowners, farmers and labourers. Their task was to tell

11. Certificate presented by the Board to women who had worked to help the agricultural war effort

*12. German prisoners of war helping with the hay harvest, 1918*

the Board when their areas needed feed, fertiliser or machinery, and to pass on official guidance which each area should follow to achieve maximum output, but until the change of government in December 1916, their work was largely unsuccessful. The Committees were slimmed down in 1917 and fulfilled their promise during the food production campaigns of 1917 and 1918.

In his *War memoirs* Lloyd George recalled: 'When I formed my administration in December 1916, I was convinced that if this country should endure to victory, it was essential that both branches of the food problem – production and distribution – should be tackled vigorously and without delay. I therefore regarded the food problem as one of our most important concerns.'

The agricultural situation had changed for the worse by then, with a bad cereals yield and failure of the potato crop, declining harvests abroad, and increasing shipping losses (with a consequent loss of cargo-carrying capacity). When Lloyd George offered Rowland Prothero the Presidency of

PUNCH, OR THE LONDON CHARIVARI—September 4, 1918.

HARVEST HOME, 1918.

WITH MR. PUNCH'S JOYOUS CONGRATULATIONS TO THE MINISTER OF AGRICULTURE.

*13. Bumper harvest, 1918*

the Board of Agriculture, with a seat in the Cabinet, he accepted and asked the Prime Minister whether he was in favour of a vigorous effort to maintain and, if possible, increase food production at home. 'Most certainly,' he replied; 'it is an essential plank in my platform.'

Both Prothero's predecessors at the Board had urged the Government to stimulate home food production, but no definite action had been taken, and unless the decline could be arrested, conditions would be even worse by the 1917 harvest and afterwards. Under the New Ministries & Secretaries Act 1916, a Minister of Food with the title of Food Controller was appointed, with the duty 'to regulate the supply and consumption of food, and to take such steps as he thinks best for encouraging the production of food . . .' Speaking in Parliament on the provisions of the Bill, Prothero welcomed the appointment and enlarged on the close co-operation he anticipated: 'My position is this: in every matter affecting the production of food the Food Controller is bound to act, under our arrangement, on my advice . . . The Food Controller has huge powers; they extend in every direction. If, for instance, a question arises of providing agricultural machinery, without the Food Controller, the Board of Agriculture is powerless. We cannot get the material, and we cannot get any implement factory released from control and set to work upon machinery; we cannot get the men exempted to work on the implements . . . but he can use powers which I have not got.'

In January 1917 the Board established a Food Production Department under Sir Thomas Middleton, to organise the expansion of crop cultivation and obtain and distribute labour, machinery, supplies of feedingstuffs and fertiliser. Sir Arthur (later Lord) Lee was appointed Director General of the reconstituted independent Department in February. Prothero's policy for 1917 was 'Back to the seventies and better! We cannot do more. I am sure that farmers will not do less'. The War Agricultural Executive Committees were given delegated powers that were 'very wide and far reaching, but Mr Prothero is confident that he can rely on the Committees to exercise them with a single eye to the national interests and with a due regard to the urgent necessity of economy in public expenditure.' The Committees had powers to inspect land, waive restrictive covenants, issue directions on cultivation and take possession of badly managed farms. They carried

*14. Lord Ernle (RE Prothero) President of the Board of Agriculture 1916–1919*

out a detailed survey of the position in each county in an attempt to alleviate some of the shortages of labour, seeds and fertilisers which might prevent an increase in output.

The supply of labour proved the greatest difficulty, 30,000 men having joined up from the land in January 1916, but thereafter the War Office co-operated with the Board as far as possible on recruitment of agricultural workers. The 30,000 were replaced by substitutes, not necessarily experienced, and unfit for army service, and men (including a number of skilled ploughmen) were released from the Home Forces for the spring cultivation. During the ploughing season farmers were allowed to hire horses from the military camps, more men were lent to help with the harvest, and prisoners of war also worked on the land. In return, the Board of Agriculture was able to help the War Office when imported meat supplies from Argentina were so low that the Home Forces had to be fed on fresh meat for five months until reserves had been built up again. The Board purchased about 160,000 head of cattle on behalf of the Army and arranged for slaughter, transport and delivery.

In January 1917 Prothero set up the Women's Branch of the Board, and a few weeks later transferred it to the Food Production Department. Its main objectives were to obtain local female help for farmers and to raise a mobile Land Army of women prepared to work full-time, go anywhere or undertake any agricultural work at the direction of the Board. The President, appealing for recruits, warned them that this was 'no occasion for lilac sunbonnets' but was comparable to life in the trenches.

The real about-turn came with the debate on the second reading of the Corn Production Bill 1917. 'Agriculture cannot be left, as it has been for more than a generation, to take care of itself. The doctrine of *laissez faire* cannot be applied to agriculture, its instruction and education as it has been in the past.' The Act, 'one of the central pillars of food production policy', guaranteed minimum prices for wheat and oats. An Order had already been issued by the Food Controller for a fixed retail price for potatoes and a maximum growers' price. The Corn Production Act also specified a minimum wage of 25/– for agricultural workers and set up the Agricultural Wages Board. It was, said the *Mark Lane Express* 'a tardy recognition of the fact that farmers were entitled to some security, and that they ought not to be asked to undertake work of the highest national importance without some guarantee against loss.'

In spite of poor weather during most of the 1917 season and shortages of labour and materials, the area under crops other than grass rose by 285,000 acres in England and Wales, compared with 1916. Already there were plans for the following year's harvest. In June 1917 the Food Production Department issued target figures to each county on the area of grassland to be ploughed and the percentage of arable land to be devoted to corn.

Certain of the Board of Agriculture's powers under the Defence of the Realm Act were delegated to Councils, enabling them to take possession of land and let it for cultivation. By such means the number of allotments in 1918 had been increased by nearly one million. Vegetables were grown in palaces and parks, and the area under hops reduced by half to allow more space for vegetables.

The Agricultural sub-committee of the Ministry of Reconstruction examined ways of increasing home-grown food supplies after the war and reported in January 1918 after the passing of the Corn Production Act. It welcomed the Act's three main principles: 'a guarantee of the price of wheat and oats to secure stability of conditions for all those who live from the land, a minimum wage to ensure his fair share of the profits of agriculture to the agricultural labourer . . . a power in reserve to the state to influence the use of land to the greatest national advantage.' The sub-Committee urged the embodiment of these principles in a wider permanent statute designed to ensure that the UK should be emancipated from dependence on imported foodstuffs and that the rural population should rise.

The net increase in the output of home-grown food from the UK, in terms of calories, was estimated by Sir Thomas Middleton as about 24% compared with 1909–

PRO PATRIA.
A TRIBUTE TO WOMAN'S WORK IN WAR-TIME.

*15. Women's war effort was widely praised*

1913, and the 1918 harvest represented a saving in shipping of some 4m tons compared with the 1916 harvest. 'Looking back', said Prothero, 'should similar necessities ever arise in the future, our national action will be guided, as well in adoption as in avoidance, by the experience gained in 1916–18.'

By 1918, farmers were subject to wide-ranging controls over the way they ran their businesses. All essential food supplies were bought at fixed prices by the Food Controller and farmers acted more or less as his agents. The old tradition of *laissez-faire* had gone – but not for good.

# FISHERIES

*WE HAVE IN THE FISHERIES A SOURCE FROM WHICH UNLIMITED SUPPLIES OF NUTRITIOUS FOOD CAN BE OBTAINED – AN INEXHAUSTIBLE STOCK OF NATURAL WEALTH... BUT THE WORK OF THE FISHERMAN AT SEA MUST BE SECONDED BY AMPLE PROVISION FOR THE DISTRIBUTION AND CONSERVATION OF THE PRODUCT OF HIS TOIL.*

Ministry of Reconstruction.
*British fishermen and the nation,* 1919

In the middle of the 19th century, herrings and oysters were cheap (a farthing each) and were eaten in large quantities. As the urban population increased, and industrialisation advanced, rivers became polluted and freshwater fish stocks dwindled. But the development of the railways improved the distribution of sea fish to inland areas, and the 'new' steam trawlers of the 1880s made it possible to extend the fishing areas to more distant grounds in the Faroes, Iceland and the Barents Sea. The industry became increasingly concentrated in large ports such as Hull and Grimsby, and the introduction of internal combustion engines into boats led to a rise in output.

The advent of war brought Board of Agriculture & Fisheries staff more directly into contact with the fisheries: the confidence of the industry in the Board 'has created an atmosphere in which questions affecting the industry and the national interest can be discussed in friendly conference with a desire on both sides to reconcile so far as possible conflicting or seemingly-conflicting interests'.*

The Admiralty requisitioned large numbers of steam fishing vessels for minesweeping and patrol duties as soon as war broke out, and recruited large numbers of fishermen to serve on these boats. The Board liaised with the Admiralty to avoid the dislocation of the industry, although it took the line that the Navy must have first call on ships and men, believing that the 'fishing industry is a great food protecting industry, and ... a fishing vessel working as a Naval unit derives from that fact an importance which as a mere fishing vessel, it never could possess'.

During the war three-quarters of the Fisheries Division staff were on active service or lent to other Departments

\* *MAF 39/7*

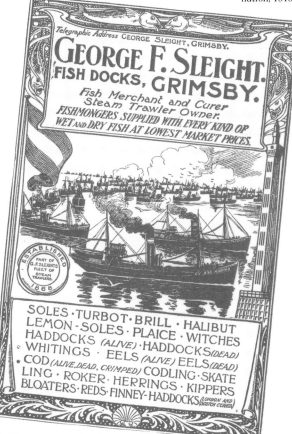

*16. Contemporary advertisement*

A GERMAN IDEA OF WAR AT SEA—SINKING FISHING-BOATS: THE BRIXHAM TRAWLER "DILIGENCE" IN PORT
AFTER BEING SHELLED BY A SUBMARINE AND LOSING HER MAINMAST.

Some time ago a "U"-boat attacked with gun-fire some of our trawlers in the North Sea. A more destructive attack was made in the Channel at the
end of November on the Brixham trawling fleet. Three vessels were sunk and others disabled. One of these latter, the "Diligence," is shown on arrival
in harbour, with her mainmast shot away and shell-holes in the hull. The submarine suddenly appeared, fired right and left, and then shot at the
boats containing the escaping crews of the sunken vessels.

*17. Fishing boats at war.*

for war duties. Those remaining worked on prevention of river and shellfish pollution, the improvement and development of small harbours, questions of charter, insurance and manning of steam fishing vessels requisitioned by the Navy. They also regulated or prohibited fishing in many areas. 'As the war has proved, fishermen and fishing vessels constitute an invaluable auxiliary arm of the Navy. If it is true that the Navy has saved the country, it is equally true that the fishing fleet saved the Navy.'

No fisheries reports were issued during World War One, for reasons of economy and discretion: 'It was necessary that the activities of the British fisherman should be veiled in obscurity illumined only from time to time by an occasional paragraph in the Press briefly recounting some tale of disaster, almost invariably accompanied by individual acts of heroism . . .' Instead, a report on *Fisheries in the Great War*, covering 1915–18, was issued in 1920 as a command paper, and written largely by Henry Maurice, the Fisheries Secretary.

The report covers the declaration of war and its effect on fishing operations, the employment of fishing vessels on naval service, and manpower problems. There are vivid,

16

often verbatim, accounts of battles with the enemy and courageous rescues. When Rowland Prothero became President of the Board in December 1916 he too was aware of the bravery and determination of the fishermen. He wrote several letters to them in 1917 and 1918 when food shortages were at their worst, begging them to 'fish all you know how . . . every landing of fish, however small, is a contribution to the food of the country' (January 1917) and again in December 1917: 'I want to make a further appeal to you to fish harder than ever . . . because the country needs every ounce of food it can get.' After the war was over, he put pen to paper once more: 'As yet, perhaps, the country scarcely knows the greatness of the debt which it owes both to those of you who have served in the Auxiliary Patrol and in the Navy proper, and to those others of you who . . . have continued to fish and to supply the country with food.'

The Motor Loan Committee was appointed in February 1917 and two months later became the Fish Food and Motor Loan Committee with a staff of 16. Help and advice was made available to fishermen, and the Fish Food section concentrated on conservation and development of those supplies which the depleted fishing fleet could provide. They saw to distribution and methods of preservation and cold storage. A grant of £50,000 was made by the Development Commissioners so that loans could be made to fishermen to install motors in their own boats, and in two years 207 engines were fitted. The Committee was wound up at the end of 1919 and many of its executive functions absorbed by the Ministry of Food. Much of its energy had gone into publicising the importance of the fishing industry in the face of widespread public ignorance ('there is a decided tendency not merely not to take the Fisheries seriously, but almost, in some cases, to treat them as a joke.')

The chief weakness of the inshore fisheries was lack of finance, and Fishermen's Co-operatives had little security to offer if loans were needed. Fishermen could borrow from the state under the Motor Loan Scheme, but the loss of a boat meant ruin. So the Government took on the whole liability for war risks and by the end of 1918, 487 boats were insured with the Cornish Fishing Vessels Insurance Society, which had been formed at the instigation of Stephen Reynolds and with the help of the Board. Stephen Reynolds became a member of the departmen-

*18. J R Clynes, Food Controller, 1918–1919*

tal Committee on Inshore Fisheries, was fisheries adviser to the Development Commission and from 1914 was Inspector of Fisheries in the South West. He and Henry Maurice, the Fisheries Secretary, often corresponded, and he wrote to Maurice in December 1917 about the possibility of forming a Ministry of Fisheries on a limited scale. Perhaps the founding of such a Ministry would prevent 'the sight of you [Maurice] ploughing along with no private secretary, a registry in another street, lost files, inadequate office service, and an administrative staff bucking along a good deal of their time with clerks' work, to make up for clerks that don't exist . . . if . . . you had at your disposal one half the money and resources the Ministry of Food is so anxious to devote to fish, you could do twice as much as they ever will . . .'

The idea of a Ministry for the Fisheries persisted, and in November 1918 a deputation went to the President, Rowland Prothero, and the *Fish Trades Gazette* published a memorandum drafted by the National Sea Fisheries Protection Association in favour of a Ministry to ensure speedy reconstruction and the general direction of a fisheries policy for the whole nation. However, the idea came to nothing despite the somewhat haphazard administration of the fisheries by a Department whose main interest, some thought, lay in agriculture. Certainly, the performance of the fishermen in time of war was praised wholeheartedly by those in power, Mr Clynes of the Ministry of Food saying in June 1918 that there were 'no heroes more extraordinary than those who have appeared among the men who furnish our vast fish supply'.

# FOOD CONTROL

*THE MINISTRY OF FOOD WAS INSTITUTED IN THE THIRD YEAR OF THE WAR AS A RELUCTANT SACRIFICE ON THE ALTAR OF INDUSTRIAL UNREST.*

Coller, F H. *A state trading adventure*, OUP, 1925

Until the end of 1916 there was no general shortage of food in Britain. Certain Government measures were taken – a Royal Commission on sugar supplies was set up at the very beginning of the war, an organisation was established to provide meat to the Army, and wheat was bought secretly to form a reserve stock. But Walter Runciman, President of the Board of Trade, did not believe in state trading and his policy, which was followed by the Government for two years, was to trust to private enterprise as far as possible to maintain civilian food supplies, and not to regulate prices. Despite the huge shipping losses already sustained by the autumn of 1916, Runciman could still dismiss the proposal for a Ministry of Food – 'this superhuman cure for all our ills' – as a joke.

But eventually rising prices and inflation, lack of cargo space for imported foods, and a bad harvest led to a change in policy, and in December 1916 the New Ministries & Secretaries Act gave authority for the creation of a Ministry of Food and the appointment of a Food Controller. Lord Devonport was the first to hold this office and started work on 26th December 1916. 'It was a post for which his long and successful business training as a great food distributor, coupled with his experience in public administration eminently fitted him', said Lloyd George, but others, notably William Beveridge, did not altogether share his views.

The Ministry started work in totally unsuitable premises in Grosvenor House. 'The ball-room was made fit for typists to type in by covering up the decorations [by Rubens], the nursery saw the birth of sugar rationing, the principal bedroom received the Food Controller, and the shades of the library formed a congenial setting for the gloomy business of deputations.'

*19. Lord Devonport, first Food Controller, 1916–1917*
*'Between Mr Runciman and Lord Rhondda fell a period of food control without principle on practical lines; a scurrying hither and thither in chase of the unapprehended consequences of ill-considered actions.'*

Lord Devonport's most lasting achievement was to control cereals through the Wheat Commission (set up in October 1916 by Runciman, but chaired by the President of the Board of Agriculture), and by the takeover of flour mills. William Beveridge, who was one of the new Ministry's most senior officials, had advocated statutory food control since the outbreak of war, together with state purchasing of imports, price fixing, and food rationing, but Lord Devonport believed in 'voluntary rationing' and appealed unsuccessfully to the nation to ration itself, then launched a food economy campaign, again without success. The voluntary approach was overtaken by events. Public anger at shortages, hoarding, and high prices grew, and even *The Times*, previously supportive, became critical. The piece of paper pinned behind the door of Lord Devonport's room in Grosvenor House seems with hindsight to be all too prophetic – 'Death to the profiteers in food and to the Food Controller unless it is stopped!' Lord Devonport resigned at the beginning of June and after a brief interregnum Lord Rhondda became Food Controller.

As William Beveridge remarked in his history of food control, 'Mr Runciman's principle of no interference at all with private enterprise suited the conditions of the first two years of war; plenty was possible and plenty was secured. Lord Rhondda's principle of complete interference was even more definitely the only one that suited the last two years of war; sufficiency, fair distribution and fair prices were attainable only by supersession of private enterprise and by that supersession they were achieved.'

During the spring of 1917 the Royal Society's Food (War) Committee had examined the whole question of the UK's food supply. Its suggestions for economising included a better recovery (80%) of flour in milling, increased economy in meat production and increased manufacture of cheese, but they were adamant about bread: 'It is impossible to ration bread without the gravest danger to the health and efficiency of the poorer element of the population, as is shown by German experience during the present war.'

Under Lord Rhondda, rationing of food and drink was enforced and all essential supplies, whether imported or home-grown, were bought or requisitioned by the Food Controller at fixed prices. Orders were made prohibiting hoarding and waste of food, and ration books issued to

*20. World War One poster*

*21. 'As a producer of problems for Food Controllers, the potato has no rival in the vegetable or the animal world.' William Beveridge*

ALIMENTARY INTELLIGENCE.

Mr. Punch. "DO YOU CONTROL FOOD HERE?"
Commissionaire. "WELL, SIR, 'CONTROL' IS PERHAPS RATHER A STRONG WORD; BUT WE GIVE HINTS TO HOUSEHOLDERS, AND WE ISSUE 'GRAVE WARNINGS.'"
[Mr. Punch, however, is glad to note that more drastic regulations are about to be enforced.]

*22. Lord Devonport, first Food Controller, believed in 'voluntary' rationing*

DAVID IN RHONDDALAND.

David. "I'M OFTEN AWAY FROM HOME. HOW DO I GET SUGAR?"
The Mad Grocer. "YOU DON'T; YOU FILL UP A FORM."
David. "BUT I *HAVE* FILLED UP A FORM."
The Mad Grocer. "THEN YOU FILL UP ANOTHER FORM."

*23. Sugar rationing was imposed in December 1917*

everybody. The Food Controller brought in outside businessmen as his technical advisers, and appointed a Consumers' Council, an advisory body with good publicity value, in January 1918, consisting of trade unionists, members of the co-operative movement, women's organisations and Ministry of Food officials. Lord Rhondda also included members of the War Emergency Workers National Committee which had been formed on the outbreak of war to campaign for legislation to help consumers withstand the effects of war more easily. It had pushed for state responsibility for the purchase, storage

and distribution of food, for vegetable allotments, for encouragement to farmers to grow more grain, a bread subsidy, and special diet programmes for mothers and children. All its proposals were eventually adopted to some extent.

A network of local Food Control Committees was set up to administer sugar rationing, continue the campaign for food economy, enforce a fixed scale of food prices, and deal with rationing of other foodstuffs. They also registered grocers and issued ration books. Food Commissioners acted as representatives of the Ministry of Food

## HOW TO WORK A TRAVELLING KITCHEN.

The announcement made by the Food Controller, that voluntary rationing is of vital importance at the present moment, has stirred an enormous amount of interest, because it is the intimate home concern of everyone in our islands.

The stocks of food in the country are low, and therefore with regard to food there are no rich people. We are all poor. Never before did a housewife's problem claim so much attention!

PACKING THE TRAVELLING KITCHEN.

All sorts and kinds of limitations are now perplexing us, and enquiries are constantly arising. Many persons fail to understand the practical questions involved, and housekeeping has become very difficult indeed. Therefore arrangements have been made by the London County Council in connection with their Women's Institutes to meet this need expressed on all sides by the establishment of Travelling Kitchens.

Free demonstrations are given during the afternoon, in five different places each week, in halls lent for the purpose. The demonstrations are held once a week in each place and the series continues for six weeks.

Ministry of Food.—No. 19.                    (0988.) Wt. 2984—1. 20000. 4/17. D & S. G 2.

*24. Many travelling kitchens were run by local Women's Institutes*

within their respective Divisions, assisted the local Committees and acted as liaison between them and the Ministry. Lord Rhondda's policy was 'to fix the prices of those articles of prime necessity over the supply of which I can obtain effective control at all stages from the producer down to the retailer ... I cannot urge too strongly on everyone the absolute need for economy in the use of all foodstuffs.' By the middle of 1918, the Ministry's staff had increased from 400 to 4,400; Lord Rhondda established a close rapport with them and was, in contrast to his predecessor, ready to delegate, gradually establishing a ministerial monopoly over the majority of the country's

food supplies.

In 1917 and 1918 there were meat shortages and two meatless days a week were declared in public eating places. A bread subsidy was introduced in September 1917 and by that November average living costs were reduced by 8%. Economies were urged on the public and Lord Rhondda was quoted in the *Edinburgh Evening Dispatch* as saying: 'I am out to win the war ... but some people seem to think that the Food Controller and his officials do not practise what they preach. I am practising what I preach, so much so that I am now less in weight and am feeling very much better. I am carrying out strictly my own regulations.' [Laughter and applause.]

Distribution difficulties led to queues for many staple foods. Queues formed as early as 5am one Saturday morning in December 1917, according to *The Times* reporter, '... over 1,000 people waited for margarine at a shop in New Broad Street in the heart of the city, and in Walworth Road ... the queue was estimated to number about 3,000. Two hours later 1,000 of these were sent away unsupplied.' Resentment grew, with the working-classes feeling that they were the only ones to suffer; there were labour disputes as the situation deteriorated, and men home from the front protested about their families' food difficulties. The local Food Control Committees in many parts of the country pre-empted the Government by devising their own rationing schemes.

Shortages intensified over the winter of 1917–18, and finally food rationing was imposed, with sugar first on 31st December and meat, butter, bacon and ham in February 1918. By July 1918 national rationing applied also to jam, margarine and lard, and there was local rationing of tea and cheese. Regulations were enforced by prosecution and fines.

By the end of 1917 many local authorities were running special nutritional programmes for mothers and children. Lord Rhondda tried to expand these into a countrywide system, and gave priority tickets for milk to nursing mothers, invalids and infants to ensure that they received their share of the dwindling supplies. 'National restaurants' already existed when Rhondda became Food Controller, with the first Government-sponsored communal kitchen opening in May 1917, and a National Kitchen Order being issued on 25th February 1918, authorising local authorities to establish and maintain such

*25. Mrs Lloyd George, Mrs Clynes and Mrs Winston Churchill lunching at the New Bridge Restaurant [one of the National Restaurants] in 1918*

kitchens in order to save food and fuel, and supply nutritious food at reasonable prices. These restaurants were subsidised, some providing cafeteria-type service, some selling takeaway meals, others being run as travelling kitchens. In the first two years of war many were opened and managed by voluntary organisations such as local Women's Institutes. Lord Rhondda approved heartily, saying in his foreword to a 1918 handbook on National Kitchens and Restaurants: 'The National Kitchen movement, which was instituted as a war measure is now becoming a part of our social organisation, and as the results already achieved are so manifestly favourable to the well-being of the people, it is almost unnecessary for me to do more than reiterate my earnest desire that local authorities should regard them as a form of insurance against a possible acute food and fuel shortage.'

Lord Rhondda died in July 1918, possibly worn out with overwork. He had been Food Controller for a little over a year and, as William Beveridge said: 'He made a Ministry of Food out of a one-man business.' He was succeeded by Mr J R Clynes MP, a member of the Labour Party, who had been acting Food Controller during Lord Rhondda's last illness.

The Armistice 'found the Ministry of Food equipped for

war and for peace . . . it controlled nearly everything that men could eat or drink without being poisoned, and many things outside that category, such as feeding stuffs and beehive sections; it was stretching out its tentacles over soap and candles, salt and aerated waters. It held unparalleled reserves of food. It had also in reserve a considered scheme for its own dissolution and was prepared to die', wrote Beveridge in his history of British food control.

There was rapid decontrol after the appointment of Sir John Beale as Permanent Secretary in September 1918. In 1919 the Cabinet Committee under Sir Auckland Geddes laid down a 'policy of progressive and comprehensive decontrol' leading to the dissolution of the Ministry. The Food Controller and Permanent Secretary resigned in January 1919 and half the staff were gone by the summer.

But at the same time food prices began to rise, and price controls were reintroduced, with coupons being issued for meat, sugar and butter in September. A general strike was threatened, and on September 26th a railway strike began. The Ministry still had large quantities of transport and other surplus war materials at its disposal, and owned a large stockpile of foodstuffs. The strike, which lasted until 5th October hardly hindered the distribution of food throughout the country and on its last day the Food Controller was able to assure the Cabinet that the country could be fed without trouble for at least another month.

On 31st March 1921 the Ministry closed its doors for the last time and its residual regulatory duties were transferred to the Board of Trade. Indispensable though it had been during war, 'the net result of its history was to furnish an overwhelming argument against any idea of establishing a system of state trading in food in normal times' said *The Times* on 14th October 1924, although it had been somewhat more generous in its obituary appreciation on 31st March 1921 of 'the biggest trading organisation that the world had ever seen. The work done by the Department . . . was of the utmost value to the military and civil population . . . To him [Lord Rhondda] belongs the credit of starting the system of compulsory rationing which, besides incidentally doing away with the intolerable burden of food-queues, did more than anything else to save the general situation . . .'

THE DEATH OF A GREAT FOOD CONTROLLER : THE LATE LORD RHONDDA.

Lord Rhondda, who died on July 3 after a long illness, became Food Controller in June 1917, and handled a difficult task with supreme success, saving the Allied cause from what might have been a very critical situation. David Alfred Thomas was born in 1856 at Aberdare, where his father kept a shop, invested his savings in collieries, and sent his son to Cambridge. After winning scholarships at Caius and Jesus, he took his M.A., and succeeded to his father's colliery interests, which he developed into the Cambrian Coal Combine, becoming also a great shipping magnate. He sat in Parliament for over twenty years, and in 1916 became President of the Local Government Board. The same year he created a Baron, and last month, a Viscount. He was among the survivors of the "Lusitania."—*Photo, Elliott and Fry.*

*26. Lord Rhondda, Food Controller 1917–1918*

# PUBLICITY AND PROPAGANDA

*27. Lord Devonport introduced
the notion of 'meatless' days*

*28. World War One poster*

We risk our lives to bring you food.
It's up to you not to
waste it.

As we have seen, food rationing was imposed late in World War One, and then only after much persuasion, as rising prices, combined with the threat of blockade by Germany led to the appointment of the first Food Controller – Lord Devonport – in December 1916. He put the emphasis on voluntary rationing, and early in 1917 appealed to the people to ration themselves, launching a food economy campaign and a 'meatless day' though without any marked success. Finally events caught up with the Food Controller: food shortages led to queues and unrest, and there were unfavourable comments in press and Parliament.

Rationing of some basic foods (but never bread) finally began in November 1917, some months after Lord Rhondda became Food Controller. He welcomed the birth of *The National Food Journal*, first published on 12th September 1917, and thereafter appearing twice monthly at 2d an issue as a 'means of giving detailed and official information in respect of the action taken by the Ministry of Food'. The Orders made by the Food Controller under Defence regulations were published throughout the country in the press, and newspapers also found room for policy announcements, while posters exhorted the public to economise on food. Food production was pushed up, allotments dug, and parks, golf courses and waste land turned over to vegetable growing.

# 3  BETWEEN THE WARS

## AGRICULTURE

*THE BRITISH FARMER WAS LEFT VERY MUCH TO HIS OWN DEVICES TO MEET THE CATACLYSM OF THE EARLY TWENTIES AND OF 1929-32.*

Murray, K. *Agriculture*
HMSO/Longmans Green, 1955

In 1919 the Board of Agriculture & Fisheries was abolished under the Ministry of Agriculture & Fisheries Act 1919 and its powers transferred to the new Minister of Agriculture and Fisheries; the remaining functions of the Food Production Department, that had achieved so much during the war, were absorbed back into the Ministry, and the Forestry Commission was established. The traditional *laissez-faire* policy towards agriculture had been abandoned during the later years of the war and by 1918 there were controls over nearly every aspect of farm work. All essential food supplies were bought by the Food Controller, and the Corn Production Act of 1917 guaranteed farmers minimum prices for their wheat.

Prices rose during 1919 and by the following April the costs of British farm products had risen 25% above the level reached at the end of the war. The Agricultural Act 1920 had laid down new (higher) guaranteed prices for wheat and oats based on 1919 averages, and subject thereafter to annual review. But in the early 1920s prices fell drastically, agriculture became a victim of the Government's post-war deflationary policies, and the Corn Production Acts (Repeal) Act 1921 cancelled the financial provisions, withdrew the guarantees and replaced them with lump sum payments. The farmers felt a sense of betrayal which lasted up to World War Two and made it hard then to win back their confidence.

By 1922 all that remained of war-time legislation was some ineffective machinery for regulating wages, a system of County Agricultural Committees occupied mainly with education, and greater security of tenure for tenant farmers. The area under cultivation in Britain shrank from 12 million acres in 1918 to under 9 million by 1926. Farms were impoverished, equipment rusted, and buildings,

29. *The forgotten industry: farmers arriving for the mass meeting at Salisbury, 5 April 1930 (the second of a series of meetings organised by the National Farmers' Union)*

hedges and ditches became dilapidated. A more gradual decline in farm prices continued until 1926 and, starting with the slump of 1929, fell a further 34% in three years. During that period MAF remained a comparatively small and static department. Its concerns included the control of pests and diseases, development of agricultural research and education, the improvement of livestock, and provision of allotments and small holdings – many of the latter provided to reward or resettle returning ex-servicemen after the war. However, work expanded considerably in the

25

The Government has restricted the imports of pigs and forced prices up to help British farmers, but so far they do not show themselves capable of producing the right sort of bacon in the right quantity at the right time.

"THERE, I KNEW WE'D FORGOTTEN SOMETHING! WE FORGOT TO CONTROL THE PIG."

*30. Marketing schemes for pigs and bacon were introduced in 1933*

late 1920s and early 30s with the Government's decision to introduce new measures to support domestic agriculture and safeguard farmers' incomes in a time of depression. Subsidies or price insurance schemes were set up for sugar beet, wheat, cattle, dairy produce and sheep. Some were administered by special bodies, such as the Sugar, Wheat and Livestock Commissions. The report of the Linlithgow Committee (appointed in 1922) on the distribution and prices of agricultural produce had led to a variety of measures and marketing schemes for improving the quality and grading of produce. Successive governments pursued various lines of reform. The first was the promotion of standardisation schemes under the Agricultural Produce (Grading and Marking) Act 1928 which enabled ministers

to prescribe standard grades, packages and packing methods and to control the use of a common trade mark known as the National Mark to denote home produce of a defined standard of excellence. By the next year, National Mark schemes were in use for eggs, beef, apples and pears. The second reform was to organise producers into co-operative marketing associations, and the Agricultural Marketing Act 1931 was designed with this object in view. Marketing Boards were established for bacon, pigs, hops, milk and potatoes under the Agricultural Marketing Acts of 1931 and 1933.

The Import Duties Act 1932 reversed traditional free trade and non-protectionist policies and imposed a general tariff of 10% on most imports including food. Tariff

31. Protesters carrying an effigy of the Archbishop of Canterbury during an unsuccessful sale of cows seized for arrears of tithes

protection was granted for a wide range of fruit, vegetables and other horticultural produce, and quota restrictions imposed on the import of bacon, ham and other meat products.

In 1934 a Royal Commission on tithe rent charge studied the whole question of the tithe burden. Years of depression had made it hard for farmers to pay this greatly resented tax to help maintain the church, and distraint orders were followed by forced sales to redeem tithe debts. In 1936 the Government abolished the charge, paid compensation to the Church and aimed to recover the money from farmers by means of tax payments over a 60-year period (due to end on the redemption date of 1996).

During the inter-war years grants for agricultural education and for scientific and technical research increased steadily. Soil surveys were carried out and techniques of pest and weed control were being mastered. Grants were made to drainage authorities, subsidies given to encourage the use of lime or basic slag and payments made for ploughing up grassland. Even so, wages were low and there was a continuing drift from the land to other industries. The numbers employed on farms dropped by 30% in the 1920s and 30s, but improvements in farming techniques meant that agricultural production increased over the same period. Gradually controls were reintroduced and guaranteed prices and protection instituted for the major farm products.

## FORESTRY

Before 1919, Britain had had no coherent national forestry policy. The agricultural revival in the middle and late 18th century, combined with a growing demand for timber for shipbuilding and periodical interruptions of imports, encouraged landowners to plant trees on an increased scale. The extension of the railway system, industrialisation and growth of cities and new commercial centres also demanded timber supplies. According to the first annual report of the Forestry Commission, imports of timber increased fivefold between 1850 and 1910, the ratio of home to foreign supplies declined and in 1914 amounted to barely 10% of the supply. Prices of imported timber rose steadily while quality declined.

Many Royal Commissions and Committees were appointed from time to time to examine methods of improving afforestation. The Board of Agriculture was made the statutory forestry authority for Great Britain in 1889, although responsibility for Scottish forests was removed by the Board of Agriculture (Scotland) Act 1911. In 1909, the Royal Commission on Coast Erosion and Afforestation recommended that a Forestry Board should be established, with powers to survey and determine how much land was suitable for afforestation, and then to acquire it. Until the passing of the Development & Road Improvement Act 1909, funds available for improvement were limited, and the Board's efforts mainly confined to the promotion of education through small grants to selected institutions.

Imports of timber were greatly affected by World War One – they took up much-needed cargo space that could be used for food so the country, thrown back on its own resources, felled old and young woods for industrial and military purposes. A national forest policy became inevitable because of the depletion of home supplies, and a sub-committee of the Reconstruction Committee was charged with considering the 'best means of conserving and developing the woodland and forestry resources of the United Kingdom, having regard to the experience gained during the war'.

An interim Forest Authority was set up by the War Cabinet in November 1918 to make preliminary arrangements for developing afforestation in the UK, and the Forestry Act 1919 established the Forestry Commission. Eight Commissioners were appointed, with the 'general duty of promoting the interests of forestry, the development of afforestation, and the production and supply of timber.'

The powers and duties of the Board of Agriculture & Fisheries, the Board of Agriculture for Scotland and the Department of Agriculture and Technical Instruction for Ireland, in relation to forestry were transferred to the new Commission, although it still had to consult the appropriate Department before taking significant decisions. Commissioners were able to purchase or lease suitable land, buy standing timber, make grants or loans to private landowners, and collect and publish statistics.

*32. Woodcutters*

# FISHERIES

*STATE AID IS NOW NEEDED IN DEVELOPING THE INDUSTRY AND REORGANISING IT BOTH FOR ITS TASK OF SECURING THE SEA'S UNFAILING SUPPLY OF CHEAP FOOD, AND FOR PURPOSES OF NATIONAL DEFENCE.*

Ministry of Reconstruction.
*Reconstruction problems no 29.*
12 June 1919.

On the question of the reconstruction of the fisheries, the Government said in 1919 that 'few men have grasped the magnitude of the work it [the fishing industry] has done . . . and few men realise the vast cargoes of fish it daily garners for our people'. The Ministry of Reconstruction's report covered all aspects of the industry, called for better distribution and preservation methods, and made recommendations for demobilisation.

Immediately after the war, the deep sea fishing industry was busy and profitable. Trawlers returned from war duty, stocks were abundant because the grounds had not been over-fished, and demand for fish was high. But the 1920s and 30s were a period of decline for this industry as for others. Over-intensive trawling out of Hull and Grimsby decimated the North Sea stock and loss of traditional markets and lack of foreign currency crippled the herring trade.

In 1933 a Sea Fish Commission was appointed under Sir Andrew Duncan to investigate all branches of the industry and make suggestions for its reorganisation. Its first report proposed a Herring Industry Board with powers to reorganise and develop the industry, and regretted the 'inescapable and major issue of redundancy' of drifters, concluding that an orderly contraction of the fleet was imperative. Through the Board, established by statute in 1935, drifters were scrapped or sold abroad. The Commissioners felt that the industry urgently needed reorganising; the export market was the predominant factor and this had greatly contracted. The Board was to be responsible for exports, would help with distribution in home markets, had powers to license boats and allocate them to particular fishing grounds, and could apply close seasons, prescribe the size of mesh for nets and regulate fishing methods.

*33. Grimsby Dock*

The trawling industry was concentrated at five big ports: Hull, Grimsby, Aberdeen, Fleetwood and Milford Haven. Hull's growth was largely due to the development of distant fishing grounds, but (with the exception of Hull) the fleet was generally old (88% being over 15 years). In 1934 it consisted of about 1,650 trawler-type steam vessels. The 1936 report of the Duncan Commission

34. Drifters

recommended that foreign landings be regulated by means of import quotas, and that a Fish Industry Development Commission should be set up. So British fishing outside territorial waters was brought under a system of state regulation and foreign imports only allowed under licence.

The plight of the fishing industry was peculiar to that industry itself – near home the stocks were dwindling, further afield the weather hindered expansion in distant waters. The annual reports of the Fisheries Secretary repeatedly called the Ministry's attention to the depression in the industry, and by 1936 there were less than 32,000 fishermen left. The final report of the Duncan Commission led to the setting up of a White Fish Commission in 1938, but this was wound up at the outbreak of war.

35. A fish sale on the beach

# FOOD

*HOW USEFUL THE YEAR OF*
*PLANNING HAD BEEN BECAME*
*MORE APPARENT EVERY DAY...*

Postlethwaite, J. *I look back*
Boardman, 1947

Although the Ministry of Food had been disbanded in 1921, a nucleus was kept in being from which the full organisation could rapidly be rebuilt, at a cost of under £2,000 a year. One Board of Trade official was retained full-time on a salary of £600 p.a. to be responsible for plans for food supply, distribution and transport,* and the Board of Trade also retained the services of the 15 Divisional Food Commissioners. Under their new name of Divisional Food Officers they were the core of a regional organisation to safeguard food supplies in the event of strikes or other emergencies. The contacts they kept up with local authorities and the food trade proved invaluable when planning of food control measures for a future war began.

In preparation during 1925 for a possible general strike, England and Wales were divided into 11 divisional areas

THE UNFAIRY GODFATHER.

Dr. Addison. "I AM HERE TO PROTECT YOU."
British Farmer. "PROTECT ME FROM WHAT? FOREIGN COMPETITION?"
Dr. Addison. "NO! NO! FROM YOUR OWN INCOMPETENCE."
British Farmer. "THANK YOU VERY MUCH."

[Under Dr. Addison's Bill, home producers are to have their output controlled, but foreigners may continue to send their produce here in unrestricted quantities. Meanwhile, as *The Times* points out, he has irritated the farmers "by unnecessary criticism of their technical ability."]

*36. CA McCurdy, Food Controller, April–June 1920*

*37. The Linlithgow Committee report led to a variety of measures for improving the quality and grading of agricultural produce*

* *MAF 60/552*

31

*38. Contemporary postcards comment on food shortages*

with the Divisional Food Officers attached to Civil Commissioners. During the General Strike itself, in 1926, telegrams were sent out on the action to be taken in the event of coal, railway and triple alliance strikes. Arrangements had also been made for daily reports on stocks, shortages, prices, movement of foodstuffs and attitude of labour, and it was proposed that Divisional Food Officers should have authority under the Emergency Powers Act 1920 to requisition foodstuffs and fix prices.

In the 1930s, quota restrictions were brought in on imports of bacon and meat to protect home agriculture. Premonitions of impending war led to the setting up of the Food (Defence Plans) Department within the Board of Trade in 1936. Henry Leon French was seconded from the Ministry of Agriculture and Fisheries to be its Director, having had previous experience in the Ministry, working on food production under Sir Arthur Lee from 1917–1919.

In this pre-war period, the small number of staff in the Department worked with all branches of the food trade and with Divisional Food Officers who had experience of World War One. Leaders in the food industry were chosen to control their particular commodities, plans were completed for the decentralisation of food stocks, and suitable people, usually town clerks, were chosen to act as Food

SPEED THE PLOUGH

*39. Ministers in the cartoon include W S Morrison, Minister of Food and Sir Reginald Dorman-Smith, Minister of Agriculture*

Executive Officers in the various local authority areas. Before war broke out, everything was prepared for, even the printing of ration books.

The experience gained in World War One was invaluable, and with hindsight there is an ironic flavour to William Beveridge's account of food control in that era, when he writes of the ministerial archives: 'There forms and circulars, reports and instructions, schemes and counter-schemes and plans for another war, all so many monuments of toiling ingenuity, lie mouldering gently into dust and oblivion – lie buried, please God, forever.'

# 4 WORLD WAR TWO
## AGRICULTURE

*WE RELY ON THE FARMERS. WE DEPEND ON THE EFFORTS THEY PUT FORTH IN THE FIELDS OF BRITAIN... TODAY THE FARMS OF BRITAIN ARE THE FRONT LINE OF FREEDOM.*

Winston Churchill. *Speech to NFU* 14 October 1940

Under the Defence of the Realm regulations the Minister of Agriculture, Sir Reginald Dorman-Smith, was given wide powers. He could regulate the cultivation and management of land, could end tenancies and, if necessary, take possession of land. On 1 September 1939 he delegated much of this power to the County War Agricultural Executive Committees, known popularly as 'War Ags'. Members of these committees served voluntarily, acted as the Minister's agents, and were responsible for carrying out his orders. They had a great deal of local autonomy and worked through a number of District Committees, assisted by a staff of experts drawn from the Ministry, universities, commercial firms, farmers and land agents. 'Understanding, experience, patience, confidence and goodwill were required for this work and they were not lacking.'

Britain entered World War Two with plans already prepared for the maintenance of essential food supplies, but depending for over 60% of her food on imports. The Ministry of Food became the sole buyer and importer of foodstuffs, and laid down price controls, so farmers were assured of guaranteed prices and markets for their produce. Other preparations included the 1937 scheme to subsidise the spreading of lime and basic slag on agricultural land to build up soil fertility, the accumulation of a reserve stock of tractors and selection of suitable men to run the War Ags. The main functions of the Marketing Boards (with the exception of milk and hops) were suspended for the duration under Defence regulations.

In 1936 the Food Supply sub-committee of the Committee of Imperial Defence had accepted a report from the agricultural departments recommending that Government policy in wartime should aim at the maximum

*40. World War Two poster issued by the Communist Party*

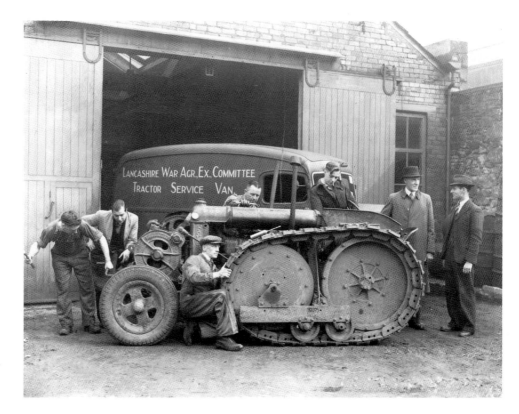

41. *War Ags organised the drive to get as much land into production as possible*

increase in home production, should make special efforts to stimulate production of wheat, potatoes, oats, eggs and sugar beet, and should maintain pre-war levels of meat, milk, and fresh vegetable production. Nevertheless, because costs and outlay on storage of feed and fertilisers were considered too high, agriculture entered the war with minimal reserves of imported feedstuffs, and incomplete supplies of fertilisers.

The home agricultural industry had to adapt to the loss of imported animal feed; the pig and poultry population were heavily reduced, and the output of foodstuffs for human consumption (wheat, potatoes, vegetables and sugar beet) increased. Government policy was to obtain more food from the land by increasing productivity of areas already under cultivation and by ploughing-up more

grassland, paying a subsidy of £2 an acre to farmers. A target of 1½ million acres to be brought under the plough was set for the 1939–40 season.

In September 1939, the Minister asked for ½ million new allotments, and a further 3 million the following year. A series of information and advice leaflets were published – the 'Grow-more' series for farmers and 'Dig for Victory' leaflets for gardeners and allotment holders, while many instructive advertisements were inserted in weekly journals. The War Ags encouraged farmers to improve their drainage systems with the help of subsidies, carried out soil analyses, and gave help with control of pests and plant and animal diseases. They allocated tractors and fertiliser rations, and set production targets for each county. Farmers' incomes rose rapidly during the first two years of war – and the money was needed to buy machinery, fertiliser and seeds. Confidence in the Government was greatly increased with the Minister's policy statement to the House on 26th November 1940. 'The Government . . .' said Mr Hudson, 'recognises the importance of maintaining after the war a healthy and well-balanced agriculture as an essential and permanent feature of national policy. The guarantee now given is meant to secure that stability shall be maintained, not only during hostilities, but during a length of time thereafter sufficient to put into action a permanent post-war policy for home agriculture.'

American agricultural machinery and equipment was sent to Britain under the Lend-lease scheme. As more machinery became available, the Ministry set up a Goods and Services Scheme in September 1941, designed to provide credit for farmers and encourage use of the services of the War Ags for ploughing, harvesting, pest destruction, hire of implements, draining, ditching, and so on. Before the war many farmers were still using horses for ploughing; by the end, they were far more highly mechanised.

A National Farm Survey was begun in 1940 to record the state of every farm in the country – its buildings, fences, drains, electricity supplies, type of soil, acreage of crops – so that the Ministry could assess its resources for the agricultural campaign. The principles were sound: to plough up as much grassland as possible, to maintain flexibility in cropping, to shift to production of food for human consumption, and to curtail output of livestock products. The farmers' main customer was the Ministry of Food, William Mabane, its Parliamentary Secretary, explained. 'Sir Jack Drummond and his colleagues tell us what are our total needs. We then ask the agricultural departments to produce as large a proportion as we think practicable and we plan to import the balance. The agricultural departments co-operate to the full and in consequence every farmer in this country, although he may not be fully aware of it, is ploughing his land, sowing his seed, taking his harvest to a nutritional pattern . . .'

The War Ags organised gangs of Land Army girls, conscientious objectors and POWs to help on the land as replacements for agricultural workers called up for active service. MAF's Press Officer, Mr F Lancum, recalled some difficulties that arose from the use of enemy labour.

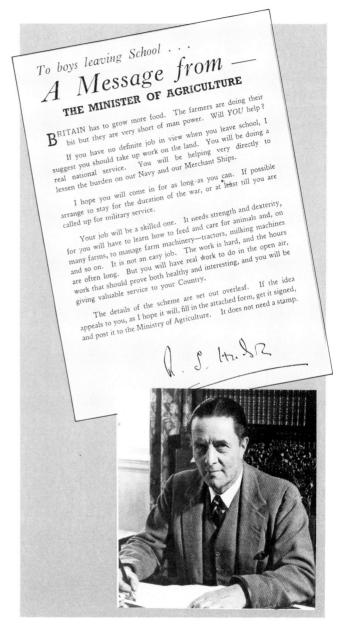

*42. R S Hudson, Minister of Agriculture, 1940–45*

35

*43. Italian prisoners of war
loading barley, 1945*

36

*44. Nearly 7,000 pig clubs flourished during World War Two*

*45. 'Dig for victory' in World War Two*

A few years before the war, six Japanese chick sexers came to Britain to practise their skilled craft. In one 16-hour day one Japanese worker sexed 'no fewer than 10,000 chicks!' In December 1941 these men were interned as enemy aliens, but the following February at the request of the Poultry Council they were released to use their professional skills to British advantage. MAF received many letters of protest, but eventually these dwindled, and a year later the Japanese were repatriated.

The general public 'lent a hand on the land' at holiday time – there were camps for schoolchildren as well as for adults, and weekend clubs for volunteers working on the land. Camps were provided in hostels and church halls, with a minimum charge for food and accommodation, and the movement really took off in 1943 with many civil servants, policemen and Home Guards working for a flat rate of 1/– an hour. On 5th May 1944 a straw stack recruiting office was set up in Trafalgar Square; it handled 450 inquiries a day, but regrettably was burnt out on 10th May.

The 'Dig for Victory' campaign began at the outbreak of war. An official rationing scheme for backyard poultry-keepers was in existence early on and by 1943–44 domestic hen keepers were producing about a quarter of the country's fresh egg supplies while, by the end of the war,

46. *WVS Rural Meat Pie Scheme, Reading 1942*

the Domestic Poultry Keepers' Council had 1¼ million members. There were nearly 7,000 pig clubs, with members feeding their pigs on kitchen waste and a special half ration of feeding stuffs. Separate pig bins became a feature of refuse collection throughout the country. Tom Williams, then Parliamentary Secretary at MAF, became chairman of the 'Dig for Victory' campaign and the Poultry Keepers' Council – its members were unofficially known as the 'backyarders' and received priority treatment. Scientists devised a formula which, when mixed with kitchen waste, would keep birds healthy and laying well, and local authorities were asked to co-operate by relaxing regulations on keeping livestock in back gardens.

Special arrangements were made for feeding agricultural workers who could not easily get home for lunch or reach any of the communal feeding centres. They received an extra cheese ration on application to the local Food Office (8oz per week in 1941, 16oz in 1942). Other classes of worker allowed this 'perk' included tractor drivers, forestry workers and charcoal burners, and Ordnance Survey field revisers. The Ministry of Food was particularly proud of its Rural Pie Scheme for distributing packed meals, pies and snacks through voluntary organisations like the WVS.

'By a combination . . . of increased home production with conservation measures, it proved possible to sustain the nation in health and efficiency on imports that, for the last three years of war, averaged only half the pre-war figures. Moreover, stocks of food in September 1945 were perhaps twice what they had been in 1939'. 'No other industry', wrote Keith Murray, the official historian of agriculture in World War Two, 'was entrusted with such a measure of self-control as was agriculture – and the trust was not misplaced.'

# FISHERIES

*NO WORDS CAN ADEQUATELY
DESCRIBE THE EXPLOITS OF
THE FISHERMEN AND THE
IMMENSE DEBT THAT THE
NATION OWES TO THEM.*

MAF. *Fisheries in war time*
HMSO, 1946

The fishermen had suffered much hardship in the 1920s and 30s, especially those who fished inshore, but the outbreak of World War Two transformed their situation immediately. Control of British shipping movements passed to the Admiralty and out of a total of around 1,030 steam trawlers in use at the beginning of the war about 816 were requisitioned at some time or other, the maximum number on naval service at any one time being about 690. The steam drifter fleet also suffered severely from requisitioning. By the end of 1939 the fishing fleet was reduced by half and the boats taken were the best and most powerful. Of these 146 – some 30% – were lost through enemy action and another 111 through other war causes; 88 skippers and 739 mates and men died.

Fishing continued but the men had to face the perils of minefields and shipwrecks. Many boats were armed with 12-pounder machine guns to protect them from air raids when fishing in grounds kept open for them by the Admiralty. Skippers of North Sea trawlers were attacked many times and several felt that every deep-sea fishing vessel should be armed. The east coast ports of Hull and Grimsby were almost eclipsed through requisitioning and the near-closure of the fishing grounds off Bear Island and Norway and the North Sea, and there was a gradual drift from the east to the west coast ports of Fleetwood and Milford Haven, with the principal grounds being fished those off Iceland, the west coast of Scotland, the Hebrides and Ireland. Fishing vessels were advised to stay together for mutual protection; steel helmets were provided for the gun crew, wheelhouses reinforced and methods of neutralising magnetic mines devised.

Fish was never rationed in wartime and remained an important item of food, although with limited supplies

*47. World War Two poster*

prices rose and from 1941 had to be controlled. By 1944 herrings cost 7d per lb and soles were 2/9d – if obtainable at all. A Fish Distribution Scheme was hastily set up by the Ministry of Food at the outbreak of war, but proved a disaster. This was a plan to decentralise the distributive side of the fishing industry, and called for the establishment of inland distribution centres with which merchants and buyers would be registered, and for the closure of the great auction markets. It was abandoned after only two weeks, because, as trawlers were recalled by the Admiralty, they landed a huge glut catch which began to deteriorate in the hot weather before it could be distributed. Sir Henry French, giving evidence to the Public Accounts Committee in 1941 recalled: 'This was the one major disaster that the Ministry of Food met with in the early days of the war. It was partly due to inadequate planning and partly due to bad luck ...' The only control that remained was the

*48. Drifter men of Britain's Royal Navy transported personnel, food supplies and mail*

registration of fishing boats and power to fix fish prices.

As a result of experience gained in the 1914–18 war, the Government arranged for insurance cover for fishing vessels, and two schemes were operated, through the British Fishing Vessels Mutual War Risks Association Ltd. and the Fishing Vessels Co-operative Insurance Society Ltd., with the Government undertaking to reinsure all or most of the risk.

Fishermen were earmarked for service either with the Navy or to follow their normal occupation. They were not allowed to enlist in the Army or Air Force and, until required for naval service, continued to fish. But manpower shortages during 1941 and 1942 (by which time they came under the Ministry of Labour & National Service) meant that they became progressively 'de-reserved'. The shortage of manpower in the inshore fisheries brought many older men back to sea. The 70-year old skipper of an inshore motor trawler was once asked by a Ministry official how he was getting on; he replied: 'Well Sir, not too good. Young Harry has joined the Navy and I have to take my uncle aboard, and he is 83 and not so nippy about the deck as I am.'

Men and vessels, mainly of the inshore fishing fleet, helped in the evacuation from Dunkirk. Motor fishing vessels were requisitioned from Brixham to the Wash, and fishermen were told to assemble at Dover, Ramsgate and Newhaven. There was no lack of volunteers but many boats were lost or damaged.

At the end of the war, requisitioned vessels were urgently needed for fishing again, and grounds closed because of the war were re-opened. Release of vessels involved extensive reconditioning, crews had to be found and the resultant increased landings at ports meant provision of more labour and transport. After the first world war there had been an overfishing problem, high prices for a few years and then a slump. The Government determined to avoid a repetition this time, sought the advice of leading scientists and announced its intention of convening an International Conference in 1946 to examine the whole problem of the fishing industry. At the International Overfishing Conference the UK proposed that mesh measurements of fishing nets and size limits of fish should be re-examined with a view to their being increased, and that the global tonnage of the fishing fleets of the different countries concerned should be reduced. Although the proposal on nets was accepted, regrettably for the fishing industry the reduction of the global tonnage of fishing fleets operating in the North Sea was rejected.

# THE MINISTRY OF FOOD

An early ministerial broadcast on rationing declared: 'It is hardly necessary to say that we work in close consultation with the Ministry of Agriculture in regard to foods produced in this country ... During the last war, in the absence of control, the index of food prices had risen 84% above the pre-war level before the first Food Controller was appointed. We are doing our utmost to prevent anything of that kind happening this time.'*

In theory, the Minister of Food advised the Minister of Agriculture on what foods should be produced and the latter was responsible for their production up to the point at which the produce left the farm. In practice, however, co-operation between the two was hampered by the fact that MAF was primarily concerned with farmers' needs and the Ministry of Food with the demands of distributors and consumers – frequently conflicting interests. This was no new situation. A memorandum on the first Ministry of Food had commented: 'During the past war the Board [of Agriculture] tended to be on the side of the farmer when his interests clashed with those of the consumer. This attitude on the part of the Board or Ministry of Agriculture – while natural and possibly correct, makes the separate existence of a Ministry of Food imperative.'**

The Ministry of Food was formed on 8th September 1939 from the Food (Defence Plans) Department of the Board of Trade. This had been set up in 1936 under Sir Henry French who subsequently became Permanent Secretary to the Ministry for the whole of the war. Detailed plans had been worked out by September 1939 for controlling the purchase and distribution of essential foods and key men had been selected to work in the Ministry in

*49. Ration book and contents*

*\* INF 1/343; \*\* MAF 60/1*

41

specialist branches such as transport and warehousing, and in the commodity divisions. Numerous meetings were held at Great Westminster House with food traders and their associations, and with national organisations. Colonial and European sources of supply were assessed and cold storage accommodation examined. Before the war over half the meat supply, nearly all fats, most sugar, cereals and flour had been imported. For the first six months of war imports were maintained at pre-war levels; thereafter many of the food-exporting countries of Europe were occupied while severe shipping losses compounded Britain's food shortages.

By March 1940, the Ministry was the sole importer of food; it had buying agencies worldwide to procure supplies and many bulk contracts with overseas governments. It also controlled distribution of home produce, and prohibited sales except to itself or to approved first hand buyers. Cattle and sheep were bought by the Ministry at fixed prices, control points created for cereals, livestock and eggs, and all milk bought at a set price by the Milk Marketing Board. Potato traders had to be licensed, and the food industries were included in the general Government policy of concentration. Manufacturers got together to produce simpler unbranded lines and fewer varieties of, for example, soft drinks and margarine. In some industries food processors continued to work on their own account, although statutory Orders laid down conditions of manufacture and sale. In other industries the Ministry retained the ownership of both raw material and finished product.

The arrival of Lord Woolton at the Ministry of Food in 1940 was hailed by one of his officials as 'an event of the greatest possible national importance. [He] had a most remarkable flair for sensing public opinion and for impressing his complete integrity of purpose and sympathy of outlook upon people generally'. Lord Woolton had exactly the right personality for getting his message of fair shares for all through the use of rationing across to the public.

When he arrived, the organisation of local Food Offices was prepared, regional officers had been appointed and the considerable quantity of printed forms was ready – including the ration books. It was 'essentially the sort of task in which the meticulous and detailed administration of a government department excelled'. But Lord Woolton saw the danger of rationing breaking down under its own

50. *Potatoes were unrationed during the war*

weight of regulations, and decided to simplify it by only rationing goods whose supply could be guaranteed, so that the Ministry would gain people's confidence that its promises would be fulfilled. 'I came to the conclusion that the only safe way was to make home agriculture the basis of our food supplies and to bring in ... only such foods as were necessary to supplement our home production and to give a balanced diet to the public'.

This was easier said than done but, with the help of Sir Henry Dale (President of the Royal Society), Lord Horder and Professor Jack Drummond, a diet was worked out for different age groups, for manual workers, fighting services, babies and nursing mothers.

The appointment of Professor Jack Drummond as Scientific Adviser to the Ministry ensured that food control was used not only to maintain, but to improve the people's diet in nutritional terms. His influence was also seen in methods of economising on shipping space by the new process of dehydration (dried eggs and milk) and by the importation of boneless meat from Argentina and folded and compressed carcasses to save precious cargo space.

A vitamin welfare scheme for young children was launched at the end of 1941, with cheap or free fruit juices and cod liver oil. As Lord Woolton said when he left the Ministry: 'We have done work of real practical social reform ... in this period of great trial we did something to establish the physical welfare of the generation that is to come ...' Energy-giving, 'filling' foods like bread and potatoes were unrationed and the Ministry promoted their use in numerous posters and recipes.

At the outbreak of war 1½ million children and invalids were evacuated, each with their emergency rations. Bulk food stocks were also dispersed from London Docks to the provinces. Smithfield and Billingsgate markets were closed and the trade transferred to the suburbs and the country. Already an anti-hoarding Order had appeared, prices of bacon, butter, cheese, tinned and other foods had been pegged at existing levels, and local Food offices opened.

The Food Offices (about 1,500) administered rationing and operated welfare schemes; they issued clothing ration books on behalf of the Board of Trade and identity cards for the Registrar-General. Other duties included the licensing of retail traders and caterers, and each Office became the local focus for food propaganda. Butter, bacon and ham, sugar and, in March 1940, meat, were the first items to be rationed; the meat allocation was based on the value of 1/10d per adult and 11d per child. Tea became rationed in July, and cheese and jam in 1941. Quantities varied – the weekly ration of meat was somewhere between 1/- and 2/2d worth, that of bacon between 4–8oz and cheese between 1–8oz. Prices were strictly controlled and consumers required to register with retailers for at least a year. 'In this country' said the Parliamentary Secretary in May 1943, 'we have deliberately chosen an equal ration for all as the basis of our policy . . . To assess the difference between the needs of different classes is a most acrimonious business and we have endeavoured to meet those variable needs in other ways. Included among these ways is the "points" scheme.'

The points scheme was for small scarce additions to the diet – often 'luxury' items such as tinned salmon or sardines, golden syrup or dried fruit. Shopkeepers built up large stocks and kept them under the counter until released by ministry Order. By using their points as they wished, consumers felt they had some freedom of choice in a world of controls.

There were a variety of emergency feeding schemes that took over during the blitz. From September 1940, a fleet of Queen's Messenger Convoys were organised by the Ministry to operate all over the country. These were self-contained units with their own water supplies, and could distribute hot drinks and snacks within the hour to meet the immediate physical needs of shocked and bewildered people. There were 21 convoys with 12 vehicles in each, including canteens and stores lorries, water tankers and kitchen vehicles staffed by volunteers – mainly the WVS. Food was given free for the first 48 hours. The Queen's Messenger Convoys (the first was donated by Queen Elizabeth) attracted good publicity – during a practice run, a sightseer was heard to say to a neighbour: 'When there's a blitz, they put wings on them things and they fly there'.

*51. A vitamin welfare scheme for young children was launched by the Ministry of Food at the end of 1941*

There were also emergency meals centres housed in schools and church halls and providing meals in large towns for those not able to cook at home because of failure of utility services in raids. Cooking depots were set up from which cooked food could be distributed in insulated containers within an area of about 20 miles. Each could produce up to 3,000 full meals in four hours. Communal meals services were developed where normal facilities were no longer available because of evacuation or transfer of workers and the resultant break-up of family life.

British Restaurants were a Ministry of Food innovation, run on canteen lines and supplying simple, nutritious food at little over cost price. They aimed to 'provide a good meal at prices from 6d to 9d in cheerful and pleasant surroundings', and were organised in collaboration with local authorities. Their name was changed from 'Communal feeding centres' after the intervention of Churchill, who wrote to Lord Woolton: 'I hope the term "Communal feeding centres" is not going to be adopted. It is an odious expression, suggestive of Communism and the workhouse. I suggest you call them "British Restaurants". Everyone associates the word "restaurant" with a good meal, and they may as well have the name if they cannot have anything else.'

The United States' Lend-Lease Act of 1941 enabled Britain to obtain supplies of food from America, although British dollar reserves were nearly exhausted. Cheese, lard and canned goods were sent over, including a variety of tinned meats with mysterious names like Tang, Prem, Mor and Spam. 'Our lend-lease food shipments to Britain in 1944 amounted to about 3% of our total food supply, but it represented to the British about 10% of their requirements ... the British diet is distinctly inferior to our own, both in quantity and variety ...' said President Truman in his 19th Lend-Lease report to Congress in 1945.

Inevitably in a period of rationing, there were those who sought to make a profit. The local Food Control Committees had powers to prosecute for any summary offence by retailers or the public against a ministerial Order, and Divisional Food Officers could prosecute others. The Enforcement Division of the Ministry, based at Colwyn Bay, exercised central supervision, the Ministry's inspectorate investigated complaints, and special staff followed up black market offences. In general, the Ministry, the 'biggest shop in the world' fulfilled its aims as described by Colonel J Llewellin, Minister of Food in the latter part of the war: 'Firstly, we have tried to lead the people rather than dictate to them. Secondly, we have acted throughout in complete harmony with those in the food trades ... At the same time we have impressed upon farmers and fishermen that they are doing just as essential work as those making or manning aeroplanes. Thirdly, our principle has been to give equal shares all round.'

52. *The Ministry of Food issued advice on using unfamiliar foods*

53. *Ministry of Food 'Food Facts' leaflet*

54. *Black marketeers were pursued by the Enforcement division of the Ministry of Food based at Colwyn Bay*

# PUBLICITY AND PROPAGANDA

*SAVE A LITTLE SUGAR, SAVE A LITTLE TEA*
*SAVE A SLICE OF BREAD EACH DAY FOR THAT BRINGS VICTORY...*

Gert and Daisy on the BBC's *Kitchen front* programme

During World War Two the publicity machine had developed to an extent where the Ministry of Food was pouring out a flood of propaganda in the form of leaflets, advertisements, posters and radio talks. Lord Woolton carried out his aim of building up public confidence in the Ministry as 'an understanding body of people whose sole aim is to help'. The message was put over with intensive advertising campaigns, such as 'Let your shopping help our shipping'. Mass Observation pointed out that Ministry propaganda had been remarkably successful, helped by the simplicity of the task it was called upon to perform. Yet up to May 1941, MoF press and poster campaigns had cost £565,000 out of a total of £1,734,000 spent on all Government press and poster campaigns (apart from those of the National Savings Committee).*

There was 'inward' and 'outward' publicity in the Ministry of Food, said Mr Shelton Smith, director of public relations during the war. 'Inward' traffic gave the Department the public's reaction to Ministry actions and policy; such information being obtained from Parliament and the general and trade press, through the weekly press conferences held by the Minister, and from local committees and the Ministry's own consumer surveys. The public were encouraged to write in, and did so on many topics. One woman wrote to Lord Woolton as 'Dear approachable Lord . . .', another told him triumphantly, but anonymously, about the unpopular National Wheatmeal Loaf: 'I got all your vitamins out and gave them to the pigs.'

The Ministry of Information's Home Intelligence weekly reports monitored the success of Government publicity – from these the Ministry would read about criticism of their advertisements and Kitchen Front talks for suggest-

55. *The National Loaf*

*\* INF 1/292*

45

ing use of foods unobtainable or scarce in some areas. Conversely, many cookery writers would check on the current food situation with the Ministry before recommending particular recipes. An intelligence report in April 1941 tells of the widespread belief that horseflesh is being incorporated in 'chicken-and-ham' rolls and suggests the authorities should 'make a clean breast of it, and publicise Lord Woolton eating it at a public luncheon'. Later that year the growing food queues are reported to be causing unrest and discontent, as it is the habit of some shopkeepers not to open until a long queue has formed, do all the day's business in a few hours and close early, to the annoyance of women war workers. But in May 1942, Lord Woolton 'continues to receive bouquets for his handling of the food situation'.

'Outward' publicity was communicated first and foremost by the Minister in Parliament, and on his tours to meet the people. As well, the Ministry issued frequent advertisements and messages on the radio telling the public about regulations, how to obtain and use ration books, how to manage food problems in wartime and eke out items in short supply, putting over the healthy eating and healthy cooking message. Much of its advice, such as cooking vegetables in very little water for a short time, was excellent. 'Food Facts' advertisements in the press taught people how to use new and unfamiliar foods like dried egg, and passed on a multitude of nutritious, cheap recipes. They did not always succeed, however; the Ministry's recipe testers were almost defeated by snoek (a barracuda-type fish from South Africa). It was generally agreed that the appearance of the fish was not very attractive. 'The colour was dark and the fish broke up into several pieces as it turned out of the can . . . when tasted raw the snoek was very firm, needed considerable mastication and the flavour was then too salty to be considered good'. The recipe most liked was mustard and cress snoek sandwiches, but the tasters found that the fish lacked flavour and the joy of the sandwich was in the mustard and cress!* Snoek was cheap (1/4½d a tin), but the public didn't take to it. The Ministry desperately issued more recipes, but by 1949 over a third of the consignment was unsold. Finally they gave up; by the end of the year, the Minister, John Strachey was admitting that it was one of the dullest fish he had ever eaten.

* MAF 256/88

56. Ministry of Food war cookery leaflet

57. Food rationing was introduced in 1940

*Recipe for piquante snoek*

| | |
|---|---|
| 4 spring onions, chopped | 2 level teaspoons syrup |
| Liquor from the snoek | 2 level teaspoons salt |
| 4 tablespoons vinegar | ½ level teaspoon pepper |
| ½ can snoek, mashed | |

Cook the onions in the fish liquor and vinegar for 5 minutes. Add the snoek, syrup and seasoning and mix well. Serve cold with salad.

The Ministry's Food Advice branch also gave tips on how to use food through its own centres and other organisations, and supplied speakers to any group wanting information about the Ministry. Domestic Science teachers were briefed with monthly bulletins on supply problems and discoveries in nutrition. Food Advice Centres were established to concentrate on personal guidance, with simple demonstrations, meetings and one-to-one advice. Their slogan was: 'Let the Food Advice Centre help *you* to win the war on the Kitchen Front' and a 1942 publicity leaflet invited people to 'drop in any time for an informal chat with the staff. You will find them friendly women, practical housewives like yourself . . . There's always something interesting going on . . . an informal talk on some current food question; news of local food supplies and prices . . .'

They also collected information about problems. The district officer for Essex and Herts, writing in October 1940 said: 'I envisage that the Food Advice Bureau should become the shop window of the Ministry not merely on this campaign but on other aspects of policy and should work in the closest co-operation with the Food Office.' Many centres were based in local Food Offices, but demonstrators also went out to local clubs and canteens, toured markets and took mobile exhibitions to outlying areas. Their aim was to fulfil the dual purpose of 'personalising' and humanising the Ministry of Food's national campaign for the right use of food and of directing interest towards the practical work being done by the Ministry generally.

The message was often put over by jingles:

'Those who have the will to win
Cook potatoes in their skin
Knowing that the sight of peelings
Deeply hurts Lord Woolton's feelings.'

and:

'Because of the pail, the scraps were saved,
Because of the scraps, the pigs were saved,
Because of the pigs, the rations were saved,
Because of the rations, the ships were saved,
Because of the ships, the island was saved,
Because of the island, the Empire was saved,
And all because of a housewife's pail.'

(Ministry of Food ad, quoted by Lord Woolton)

The film section prepared 30-second 'Food flash' spots for cinemas, and the Ministry of Information produced instructional cookery films for the Ministry.

Radio was widely used, and included talks by the Radio Doctor (later to be Parliamentary Secretary at the Ministry), a Food Production Brains Trust, or a Ministerial broadcast to the Empire. There were regular Kitchen Front chats by well-known writers or actors, giving news of the latest food prices, new items reaching the shops, Ministry information and, of course, more recipes.

The Ministry of Agriculture, under R S Hudson and Tom Williams also produced massive publicity. Simple 'Dig for Victory' leaflets were issued, and the 'In your garden' broadcasts were aimed at a large section of the community, demonstration allotments were started in open spaces and the Ministry had its own plot in Hyde Park. Campaigns for increased food production exhorted the farmers to plough the fields and to 'Raise more food for man and beast'. A New Year message from Tom Williams to farmers and farm workers continued the theme after the war was over. The 'Eat more potatoes' campaign was launched in 1940 and Potato Pete and Dr Carrot became familiar figures.

'Dig for victory' said the Minister, R Dorman-Smith, in an early leaflet: 'Let this be the slogan of everyone with a garden: of every able-bodied man and woman capable of digging an allotment in their spare time.' By 1942, according to a Ministry of Information *Home Front Handbook*, there were 1¾ million allotments – almost double the pre-war figure, and between two and three million private gardens were contributing to the home production effort. Parks, golf courses and tennis clubs were transformed into vegetable gardens, and in larger towns Horticultural Advisory Committees were established by local authorities to help allotment holders. Many people joined Pig Clubs ('Pigging for Victory' was a slogan coined by one bright local paper for the movement!), and others kept poultry with the blessing of the Ministry.

Agricultural radio had started regular broadcasts in 1934, with its avowed aim to provide the agricultural community with technical information and keep farmers and others up to date with market prices and trends, and new developments in the industry generally. The intention was to stimulate interest and ideas and to lead people to seek more detailed knowledge from sources such as the advisory service, the farming press, and technical literature. Radio programmes played a significant part in the agriculture and food war effort. A memo on 'Farming Today' dated November 1939 remarks: 'At the present moment, the Ministry of Agriculture as the Department responsible for the Home Food front are getting an excellent broadcast service. But this is the result of independent action on our part and the exploitation of our close association with the agricultural and horticultural world built up in peace-time . . . although it is war-time, I think it would be most unwise for us to become agents of Government policy'.

Writing in 1941 on the then current position of agricultural broadcasting John Green, director of agricultural broadcasts, said that national programme policy was subject to an element of ministerial influence, though this was never oppressive. A special liaison to meet the new position had been agreed in November 1939 by the Director General and the Minister for Agriculture, and in October 1940 a Broadcast Planning sub-committee was formed under the chairmanship of Anthony Hurd as a branch of the Minister's Publicity Committee. By 1942 the Corporation had become one of the main channels of official communication with farmers, and that September, as a result of increasing official directives, a news and announcement item: 'Farm Record' was added to the national programme.

The Broadcast Planning Committee consisted of people with practical experience of broadcasting who brought to the BBC a wide range of editorial advice and criticism and also the services of MAF's publicity machine. 'Thus we managed jointly to temper with reason a flood of official direction, in such a way that the morale and intelligence of the industry was improved rather than impaired.'

*58. Home-grown fruit for jam took the place of imports*

# 5 MAFF POST-WAR AGRICULTURE

*...AND THE GOVERNMENT PROPOSE TO ESTABLISH AS AN ESSENTIAL AND PERMANENT FEATURE OF THEIR POLICY FOR FOOD AND AGRICULTURE A SYSTEM OF ASSURED MARKETS AND GUARANTEED PRICES FOR THE PRINCIPAL AGRICULTURAL PRODUCTS...*

Tom Williams. *Speech to the House,* November 1945

By the end of the war much more land was under cultivation, the farming industry was almost entirely mechanised, and farmers were subject to a great deal of control. Britain's foreign exchange reserves were severely depleted, Lend-Lease had been suspended in August 1945, and large areas of the world faced severe food shortages so that food which Britain might have imported had to be diverted to these areas and rationing had, perforce, to continue.

British farmers were again urged to increase their output. In August 1947 Prime Minister Attlee announced a programme designed to raise the net agricultural output of the UK by 20% over the next five years (50% over pre-war); in 1952 the Conservatives increased this target figure to at least 60% above pre-war. An intensive publicity campaign was launched to recruit 200,000 volunteers for agricultural camps during 1948, and press advertisements, leaflets and posters urged schoolchildren and their teachers to 'lend a hand on the land at a farming holiday camp' and to help with potato and fruit picking. Expansion was needed in numbers and output of livestock, and in acreages of cereals and potatoes.

Tom Williams became a popular Minister for Agriculture in the 1945 Labour Government. His major priority was to maintain the momentum of food production and he announced his plans in the House on 15th November 1945: 'The objective will be to promote a healthy and efficient agriculture capable of producing that part of the nation's food which is required from home sources at the lowest price consistent with the provision of adequate remuneration and decent living conditions for farmers and workers . . .'

*lend a hand on the land*

*at a farming holiday camp*

59. *Agricultural output targets were increased after the war and volunteers desperately needed*

(2490) *FARMER and STOCK-BREEDER, December 31, 1946*

ISSUED BY THE MINISTRY OF AGRICULTURE AND FISHERIES

## *A*
# *New Year Message*
### from the
# MINISTER of AGRICULTURE
### to Farmers and Farm Workers

WE must still go all out to feed as many of our own people as we can from our own soil. World food prospects for 1947 give no cause for optimism, and much coarse grain normally available to livestock feeders will have to be used for human food.

We cannot expect more than our fair share of world food exports; what we get will certainly fall short of what we desire.

The Nation will need all the bread grains, potatoes, sugar-beet and vegetables that you can possibly grow. Milk is vital to national well-being. Every livestock producer must aim at the highest degree of self-sufficiency in feeding stuffs, so as to keep up milk supplies and, at the same time, have as much feed as possible to spare for pigs, poultry and other stock.

I know your difficulties; but I know, too, that your country can confidently rely on you, as it did in time of war, to surmount them and to make your full contribution to the Nation's food supplies.

*Tom Williams*

MINISTER OF AGRICULTURE AND FISHERIES

*60. Agricultural production was pushed up in post-war years*

February 1945, were to continue and in order to give farmers assurance of stable prices, there was to be a rolling programme of price fixing by the Government. The assurances on guaranteed prices and assured markets were made statutory by the passing of the landmark Agriculture Act 1947, as were the annual reviews of the general economic conditions and prospects of the industry.

MAF was empowered to impose supervision orders on those who did not manage their land efficiently, an independent Agricultural Land Tribunal was set up to hear appeals on dispossession, and the Agricultural Statistics Advisory Committee was established.

The Agriculture Act 1947 also provided for a 'permanent' system of County Agricultural Executive Committees to continue the work of the War Ags which had contributed so much to wartime food production. As before, the Minister delegated certain functions to them, and members were appointed by him, the majority being chosen from lists submitted by the NFU, the Country Landowners' Association and the farm workers' unions. Many of the old members continued to serve, but the staffs attached to the Committees became civil servants employed by the Ministry. In the immediate post-war period these Committees helped in the continuing expansion of home food production, but gradually their work was reduced by the ending of rationing of animal feedstuffs, the winding-up of mobile labour gangs, and the reduction of trading services such as machinery hire. Their supervisory powers over farmers in cases of inefficient estate management were repealed in the Agriculture Act 1958.

Between the wars advisory work had been carried out through County Councils and the agricultural departments of universities and colleges. These were united within the National Agricultural Advisory Service (NAAS) in 1946, set up as a result of the growing awareness during the war of the significance of technical advances in improving agricultural production. The Service was organised in eight regions with about 500 general advisers, and also specialists within the counties. It provided free technical advice to farmers and also gave lectures and demonstrations, as staff kept in touch with research institutes so that they were informed of all the latest scientific findings. Research and development work was carried out on NAAS experimental husbandry farms and horticultural stations, and, in addition to giving technical advice, district advisory officers also assisted with applications for improvement grants.

As early as the 1950s, NAAS's farm management advisers were trying to win acceptance of the idea of a business approach to farming problems and the development of business management techniques. In 1963 the Farm Management Department was established within NAAS and techniques were developed for whole farm analysis and individual crop and livestock enterprise costing. By the end of the decade many enterprise recording schemes had been computerised, for example, the Poultry Scheme in 1964 and the Dairy Management Scheme in 1967.

During the 1950s (and with a new Conservative Government taking office in 1951), the system of administrative controls was gradually dismantled. Derick Heathcoat Amory became Conservative Minister of Agriculture in 1954 at a time when agricultural policy was still firmly based on the 1947 Act. 'When we took office,' he recalled, 'farmers were still being told largely what to grow, bulk purchase of food by the Government was still the order of the day and ration books were still with us – six years after the end of the war. The whole business of food provision was hindered and throttled by Government controls, which were vital in wartime, when food was scarce, but no longer necessary. Our aim was to get rid of these controls as quickly as we could. And within a year or two we had done that.'

In December 1956 he wrote to Lieutenant-General Sir Ian Jacob, Director General of the BBC, about the possibility of having a regular agricultural programme when the second TV channel became available: 'I regard television as the most promising medium for two important national tasks – increasing the mutual understanding and knowledge between town and country and spreading amongst farmers the vital doctrines and techniques of improved technical efficiency.'

Sir Ian replied in April 1957: 'Your Department is in a unique position from our point of view not only in representing the Government in the agricultural sphere, but also in being an impartial and disinterested body whose activities cover the whole field of rural life.' He went on to describe the projected TV farming programme, which 'will be directed primarily to farmers and farm workers, and will be a medium for technical education which I believe will prove of revolutionary importance at the present time'.

A BBC Press Notice the same month promised that the new Agricultural Television Service would be an extension of the regular sound broadcasts which had been established since 1934. It was to be a national service, organised in Birmingham, and the Corporation believed that 'the educational potential of television is so great that it can make an immediate contribution to technical efficiency on the farm and the lowering of costs in production'.

On the radio side, as well as the regular farming programmes, a new series had been launched some years before. 'The Archers' was originally intended as a programme presenting 'an accurate picture of country life' that would 'eavesdrop on the many problems of living that confront country folk in general'. Accuracy was essential – 'for instance, should any important country matter be discussed in the House of Commons, we should include the natural reactions of our characters to this subject.'

The BBC was assisted in the production of this, as with other farming programmes, by the central and regional Agricultural Advisory Committees which had members drawn from all sections of the industry – one member wrote to producer Godfrey Baseley in 1952 about 'The Archers': 'I see in it not only a most marvellous medium for getting the country across to the town, but also for getting increased agricultural production.' The MAF Press Officer of the day [1953], A D Bird, commented on the 'value of the programme to the Ministry for getting topical news items across to farmers'. He felt that the Ministry could help by keeping Mr Baseley in touch with future policy, by supplying news items as they arose and by giving advice on technical matters. But – wrote Godfrey Baseley – 'we have to watch it very carefully so that we are not accused of being a vehicle for propaganda'. Today things are different: 'We try to get some agriculture into every episode, but it's woven in much more carefully than it used to be . . . in the old days Dan and Phil Archer would just read Ministry handouts and it stuck out like a sore thumb.'

# FISHERIES

*THE FLECK REPORT ON THE FISHING INDUSTRY IS FIRST CLASS, SO FAR AS IT GOES. IT MAKES NO BONES ABOUT THE FACT THAT, FOR YEARS THE INDUSTRY HAS FAILED TO ADAPT ITSELF TO CHANGING CIRCUMSTANCES.*

The Times, 13 January 1961

The years immediately after the war were busy for deep-sea fishermen. Trawlers returned from war service and demand for fish remained high because other food was scarce. But in 1949 the industry was again in trouble; prices fell below production costs and many trawlers were laid up. Government help was forthcoming in the provisions of the Sea Fish Industry Act 1951, under which a White Fish Authority was appointed, somewhat on the lines of the defunct pre-war White Fish Commission.

The Authority was able to regulate, reorganise and develop the industry. It could carry on research and experiments or give financial aid to other research workers. In its first years it devised and operated a quality control scheme at Hull, examined mechanised landing and fish handling at Grimsby and collaborated with Torry and distant water trawler owners in experiments on freezing fish at sea. From the outset the Authority worked closely with Torry and funded much research work. In the 1960s they collaborated on the production and test marketing of prepacked chilled fish, and on consumer trials of the best methods of presenting and distributing packaged fish.

The White Fish & Herring Industries Act 1953 gave the White Fish Authority and the Herring Industry Board power to make grants and loans for inshore, near and middle-water vessels, and a further Act in 1957 authorised grants for converting coal-fired engines to oil-fired steam propulsion. A subsidy on white fish (except for the distant-water fleet) had been paid since 1950, for herrings since 1957, and was extended to the distant-water fleet in 1961.

The Fleck Committee report recommended in 1961 that financial aid should continue for the whole fishing industry, both by operational subsidies and by grants and

61. *M Graham, Lowestoft Fisheries Laboratory director 1946–1958, a practical man*

*62. Cod War 1975/76: Gunboat* Tyr *rams Frigate* HMS Yarmouth

loans for the construction and modernisation of vessels for a period of 10 years. The industry's future prosperity depended on modernisation of its vessels and rationalisation of its structure, with increasingly close connection required between the catching, processing and distributive sides. This was accepted by the Government with the intention that the trawler sector should become self-supporting within 10 years, and the Sea Fish Industry Act was passed in 1962.

Local Sea Fishery Committees regulated the inshore fisheries and were able to make by-laws (subject to Ministry approval) to restrict or forbid any particular method of fishing, control discharge of harmful substances into the sea and keep down the numbers of predatory fish or marine animals. The Sea Fisheries Inspectorate was the link between the Fisheries Department and the industry,

and maintained contact with the principal deep-sea fishing ports and the many small harbours along the coast. Inspectors kept in touch with associations and unions, the Fishery Protection Squadron of the Royal Navy and officers of local committees, and enforced the legislation.

During this period there were several attempts at concerted action to conserve fish stocks. The Overfishing Convention of 1946 applied to the North Atlantic and was ratified in 1953, a permanent Commission being set up and acting on the recommendations of the Convention. In 1949 an International Commission for North West Atlantic Fisheries was established and the two Commissions laid down minimum mesh sizes for trawls for different species by regions during the 1950s; minimum landing sizes were linked roughly to the smallest mesh size enforced. By the end of the decade similar rules were established for all the

53

trawling fleets in the North Atlantic, but nevertheless the North Sea herring fisheries failed in the mid-1950s and 60s. Enforcement was put on an international footing in the late 1960s and a system of Total Allowable Catches and national quotas was introduced.

The Fisheries Department was also greatly concerned with international fisheries problems, particularly with fishing limits. Between 1950–58, for example, Iceland unilaterally extended her fishing limits from three to 12 miles, and this gave rise to the first of three 'Cod Wars' because British deep-sea fishermen had traditionally fished in this zone and were now excluded. On each occasion fishery protection frigates provided 'havens' for British trawlers and protected them from arrest by Icelandic gunboats.

The first Cod War was settled in March 1961, when Iceland's fishing limits were extended to 12 miles. The second Cod War lasted from 1971–73 and the third from 1975–76. The disputes finally ended in 1976 with Icelandic rights to a 200-mile zone being recognised, and a six-month agreement that resulted in British fishing effort in those waters being limited to an average of 24 trawlers a day. Similar regimes appeared over the rest of the world's continental shelf at this time and free access to grounds off Newfoundland, Greenland, Norway and Bear Island was also lost, although access to limited opportunities in those grounds was subsequently regained under arrangements negotiated by the European Community. This factor above all else led to the drastic reduction over the next 10 years of the British distant-water fleet.

Under the River Boards Act 1948, each river system in England and Wales was placed under an authority responsible for controlling salmon, trout and freshwater fisheries, land drainage and river pollution. Other Acts, dating from 1923, regulated and controlled the salmon and freshwater fisheries, prohibited destructive methods of fishing and laid down the times during which fish could be caught and sold. The operation of these acts was reviewed in 1961 by a Committee chaired by Lord Bledisloe and certain legislative changes followed. The structure of the water industry was changed radically under the Water Act 1973, which created 10 water authorities in England and Wales to take on water supply and sewage functions and the functions of the former river authorities, including the regulation of salmon, trout, eel and freshwater fisheries.

The Act placed on the water authorities the statutory duty to maintain, improve and develop the fisheries in their areas, and the Salmon & Freshwater Fisheries Act 1975 incorporated this obligation. For these purposes the water authorities have powers to make byelaws, orders and take enforcement action. Their powers were strengthened by the Salmon Act 1986 which, in addition to modifying the 1975 Act, created offences of handling illegally caught salmon and provided for salmon dealer licensing schemes to be established.

Fisheries research resumed at Lowestoft after the war, with two vessels, the *Sir Lancelot* and the *Platessa* in service by 1947, joining the *Onaway* which had been acquired in 1933. In 1947 too, a laboratory was set up in Lowestoft to assess the consequences of permitting low-level radioactive waste disposal into the Irish Sea from the proposed nuclear fuel reprocessing plant at Windscale then under construction. From the first this was an integral part of MAF's Directorate of Fisheries Research but, as was the case with the physical and chemical oceanographers, the staff were dispersed in various parts of the town and in 1951 the takeover of 'a derelict building known as the Grand Hotel' was mooted. In 1955 all Lowestoft work except the studies of radioactivity in the marine environment moved to that site and in 1982 a new wing was added, principally to house the radiological section. Much of the work was carried out at sea, and from 1948–70 a purpose-built, distant-water research vessel, the *Ernest Holt* was used for research in the Barents Sea, off Greenland, the White Sea and Spitzbergen. These biological, physical and chemical studies were complemented by shore-based studies of fish behaviour and the development of a sampling scheme at all main fishing ports that together gave scientists the ability to assess the effects of fishing not only on distant-water stocks, but also the fish stocks of the seas around the British Isles.

The replacement of the *RV Sir Lancelot* in 1961 by *RV Clione*, the second vessel built to MAFF specifications, was an important milestone in the development of these North Sea, Channel, and Irish Sea programmes of work. Another was the increased awareness in the UK as a whole during the 1960s of the importance of environmental protection. This has been reflected by greater emphasis in DFR's work since then on understanding and monitoring what was happening in the marine environment as a consequ-

63. RV Cirolana, *fisheries research vessel, launched 1970*

ence of marine activities other than fishing. In 1974 MAFF acquired statutory responsibility under the Dumping at Sea Act 1974 for the protection of the marine environment from pollution caused by the sea disposal of waste. These powers were recently strengthened with the enactment of Part II of the Food & Environment Protection Act 1985.

Before World War Two, the UK was one of the largest whaling countries. Eight expeditions were made by factory ships during each Antarctic summer, and whaling stations operated from South Georgia and South Africa. After the war (during which factory ships had ferried fighter planes across the Atlantic – and suffered major losses), three new vessels were built and operated with the land stations until 1960. The International Whaling Commission had been set up in 1946 to 'provide for the conservation, development and utilisation of the whale resources' with 15 member nations whose catches accounted for about 90% of the world catch. Britain ceased all whaling activities in 1963, but has remained an active member of the Commis-

sion. In recent years the UK has taken an increasingly conservationist line within the Commission in concert with other like-minded countries and has succeeded with them in securing a moratorium on commercial whaling.

Powers to control fish diseases date back to 1937 when the Diseases of Fish Act prohibited the import of live salmon and trout and granted Ministers powers to control the movement of fish to and from any sites infected with serious fish diseases notifiable under the Act. Today these controls mainly focus on those diseases affecting salmon and trout, the basis of our successful freshwater fishing industry.

The Ministry's commitment to controlling fish disease was confirmed with the establishment of the separate Fish Diseases Laboratory at Weymouth in 1969; this now has an international reputation. Controls were reinforced by the Diseases of Fish Act 1983, which enabled the Fisheries Department to introduce a system of fish farm registration.

# FOOD

In a message to Ministry of Food staff before the war ended, Colonel Llewellin praised their achievement but was realistic about the future: 'Victory will bring new problems, for unfortunately we know that there will be no immediate prospect of plenty. As supplies improve, and labour comes back from the services and war-industries, we shall gradually be able to unwind many of the numerous controls which have had to be imposed on producers, on the trade, and on consumers.'

He was right about the food shortages, but not about relaxation of controls. The Hot Springs World Food Conference of 1943 had foreseen that a world shortage of food following the Armistice would make it necessary to organise imports on a national and international scale, continue rationing and controlled distribution, and promote a sustained high level of agricultural output. In February 1946 a cut in bacon, poultry and egg rations was announced, in April the size of the 1 lb and 2 lb loaves was reduced. Lend-Lease had been abruptly ended in 1945 and it was the job of the Ministry, under its Labour Ministers Sir Ben Smith and John Strachey to reduce dependence on dollar imports of food.

The Ministry was no longer as popular as it had been under Lord Woolton. Favourite items such as canned meat and fish disappeared, to be replaced by whalemeat in 1947, memorably described by Susan Cooper in her essay 'Snoek piquante' as a 'curious powdery-textured substance resembling a meaty biscuit, with overtones of oil.' Snoek followed later that year and the Ministry's kitchens devised all manner of recipes (see page 47) to persuade people to eat it, but with very little success. The Ministry was still responsible for buying food in bulk and distributing it to retailers through local Food Offices. Ration books remained in force for basic foods, with the addition of personal points for sweets and points for many canned goods and dried fruit.

To conserve wheat stocks, the extraction rate of flour was raised again, and in July 1946 rationing of bread, cake, flour and oatmeal was imposed, with coupons known as 'Bread units'. A bad potato crop in 1947–48 forced the Government to introduce a restricted allowance of 3 lbs a week to the consumer, and in 1947 milk was also in short supply. Mr Strachey was unpopular with both the press and Parliament.

There were many complaints from housewives during this age of austerity. A British Housewives' League had been founded in 1945 as a non-party organisation concerned with housewives' grievances. Thousands joined in 1946 when Sir Ben Smith decided to cut off supplies of dried egg; they held a mass meeting and forced him to reverse the policy. Bread rationing provoked more protests and was abandoned in July 1948, although rationing of butter, margarine and meat continued until 1954.

In 1947 the Ministry of Food set up the first Food Standards Committee which in turn appointed sub-committees to deal with food additives and contaminants. A Food Additives and Contaminants Committee was subsequently established in 1964. Both committees assessed current scientific evidence and advised on the necessity for regulations to be made under Section 4 of the Food & Drugs Act 1955. This Act sought to ensure the safety and wholesomeness of food for the consumer, to prevent misleading labelling or advertising of food, and to protect the honest trader.

During the war and immediately afterwards, the Ministry of Food made a number of long-term agreements with overseas governments and with producers' organisations to secure future supplies of basic foodstuffs such as meat and sugar. The General Agreement on Tariffs and Trade (GATT) was concluded in 1947 and MAF was deeply involved in negotiations and discussions under the GATT, in OEEC, OECD and EFTA. International agreements regulated production and trade in individual commodities; a series of sugar agreements dated back to 1931 and there were others on wheat, coffee, cocoa, tea and bananas, several of which are still administered by MAFF divisions. The External Relations division took part in negotiating international trade agreements before the UK's accession to the European Community and is now involved with the Lomé Convention, the Food and Agriculture Organization and the World Food Council.

The war left the nation more 'food conscious' than before, and the *National Food Survey*, started during the war, continued to provide information not previously available, on food budgets and diets. Another legacy of the war was the close contact maintained between the food trades and the Ministry. Although food rationing ended in 1954 and wartime controls were gradually dismantled, there was still a quantity of 'food work' to be done, but the Ministry would soon have too little work to justify its retention as a separate Department.

There were several options – the work could be split among several other Departments, or it could be absorbed into the Board of Trade, an idea popular with the retail trade and with the Ministry's Parliamentary Secretary, the ex-Radio Doctor Charles Hill who believed that 'in essence it had been a consumer's organisation and I doubted whether the consumer's interests could be fully protected if what remained of the Ministry of Food passed to the Ministry of Agriculture and Fisheries – the main alternative.' But the Board of Trade already had a heavy workload, and it was felt that the Ministry should be amalgamated with MAF, with one Minister responsible for looking after farmers, fishermen and consumers – for every link in the food chain. Lord Woolton, as Lord President of the Council was given the task of relating the affairs of both Departments with a view to their eventual union, and the decision on the merger was announced in October 1954. In the interim period the then Minister of Agriculture and Fisheries, Derick Heathcoat Amory, combined that post with that of Minister of Food.

The merger was not popular with *The Times*: 'The worst of the possible alternatives has been chosen. If there could not be a separate Minister of Food, his remaining responsibilities should have gone anywhere rather than to the Minister of Agriculture. It is asking too much of any Minister to be able to hold the balance fairly between the interests of the consumer and the powerful agricultural interest.' *The Grocer* grieved for Dr Hill who, 'as surviving Parliamentary Secretary has to assist in the transfer of the remnants of the Ministry of Food into the grip of that octopus of ill-repute, the Ministry of Agriculture.' Attlee asked in the House whether the Prime Minister 'gave consideration to the point that the Ministry of Food was essentially placed there to protect the consumer and has now been joined with the Ministry of Agriculture? Is not the amalgamation rather like that of the young lady and the tiger?'

However, the amalgamation was finally made official by an Order in Council, passed in the House by 207 votes to 172, and on 12th April 1955, the Ministry of Agriculture, Fisheries and Food was born. It was said that no one could even agree on a name for the new Ministry, and its eventual title was chosen by the Prime Minister.

In the 1960s and 70s, the Ministry's sponsorship of the food and drinks industries was greatly affected by the general increase in prices. Successive attempts were made during the period to control inflation, the work of the National Board for Prices and Incomes being closely followed by the establishment of the Price Commission and formulation of the Price Code. MAFF participated actively in the development and application of price policy, much of the effort being directed to adapting policies to the particular circumstances of the food and drinks industries. From 1979 Government policies moved towards reduced intervention, with the current emphasis being on removing the burden of regulation from industry and allowing market forces to operate freely. In the 1970s the Ministry was also concerned with maintaining food supplies in the face of industrial action and shortages, in particular during the energy crisis and the road haulage strike some years later.

# PART II

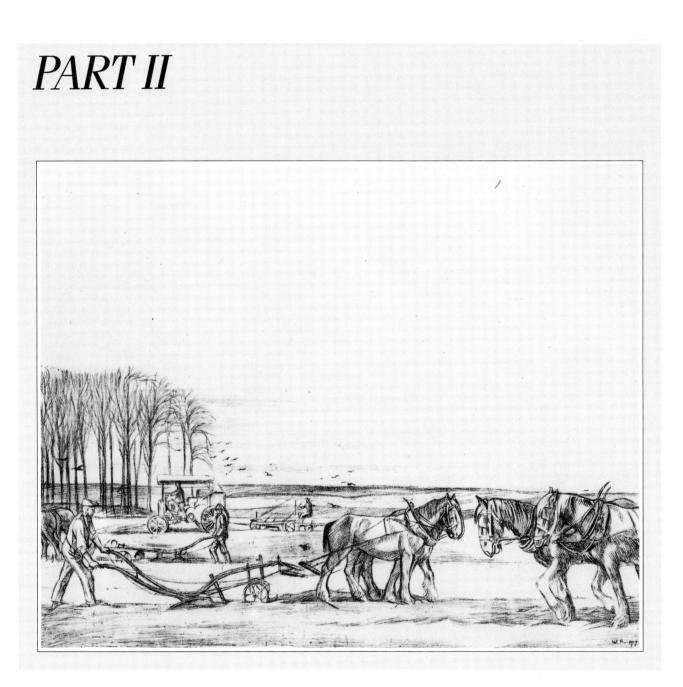

# 6 ANIMALS AND LAND
## ANIMAL HEALTH

*A CONTAGIOUS AND
INFECTIOUS DISORDER... HAS
LATELY APPEARED AND NOW
PREVAILS AMONG CATTLE
WITHIN THE METROPOLIS AND
IN THE NEIGHBOURHOOD
THEREOF, AND IT IS EXPEDIENT
TO TAKE MEASURES FOR
PREVENTING SUCH DISORDER
FROM SPREADING...*

*Order in Council*, 1865

In the summer of 1865 a cargo of cattle shipped from the Baltic was the probable source of one of the worst outbreaks of animal disease ever seen in Britain. Known as cattle plague or rinderpest, the infection spread rapidly from Islington to the whole country. Prayers were said in churches, and in January 1866 the Archbishop of Canterbury wrote to the Home Secretary begging for the appointment of a day of 'national humiliation' to implore divine aid. This request was turned down and statutory methods were employed instead. The Cattle Disease Prevention Act 1866 was rushed through Parliament in a week and became law in February. This ordered the slaughter of infected animals by local authorities, restriction of animal movements, disinfection of premises, and compensation for owners. The plague claimed about 400,000 cattle, but the country was finally declared free from rinderpest in September 1867.

The Cattle Plague Department, which had been established in 1865 to deal with the epidemic, began its life as a branch of the Home Office but was transferred to the Privy Council in 1866. Four years later its name was changed to the Veterinary Department and staff continued to administer a series of acts for the control of other animal diseases such as foot-and-mouth and pleuropneumonia (for the eradication of which the Board of Agriculture was made responsible in 1890), sheep scab and glanders. Veterinary Inspectors were employed at ports of landing and had wide powers of detention and slaughter, while the number of ports at which animals could be landed was drastically reduced.

In 1883 the Department took over publication of the annual agricultural statistics from the Board of Trade, and again changed its name – to the Agricultural Department.

PUNCH, OR THE LONDON CHARIVARI.—November 18, 1865.

BEEF?
FOURTEEN PENCE
A POUND
Ha Ha!

THE DEMON BUTCHER, OR THE REAL RINDERPEST.

*64. Rinderpest (or cattle plague) claimed the lives of 400,000 cattle in 1865–67*

It became the Veterinary Department of the new Board of Agriculture in 1889 and its main function was to control the spread of, and eradicate animal diseases – initially cattle plague but closely followed by swine fever, rabies and anthrax. In later years duties such as meat hygiene, artificial insemination and the import and export of live animals were added. Authority to kill foot-and-mouth diseased animals was transferred from local authorities to the Board in 1892.

In that year the number of rabies cases had fallen so low that the Board revoked the orders for muzzling dogs, and cases started to increase again. A Departmental Committee on dog laws reported in 1897: 'We think . . . that the time has come and that the circumstances are opportune for the Board of Agriculture to make a determined and systematic attempt to stamp out rabies.' A centralised system of muzzling was imposed and the disease was eliminated from the country for the first time in 1902, although the policy 'was the subject of a storm of hostile criticism'. In 1918 rabies was reintroduced, probably by a dog smuggled in by a returning soldier, and 319 cases were confirmed before it was again eliminated in 1922. Apart from two isolated cases in 1969 and 1970, associated with dogs recently released from quarantine, the country has remained rabies-free. These last cases led to a wide-ranging review into the rabies import policy which endorsed the need for a six months quarantine.

The consolidating Diseases of Animals Act 1894 gave the Board of Agriculture wide discretionary powers to handle any animal disease and make any Orders it considered necessary. The Board was the central authority, and county councils and borough councils were appointed as the local authorities to execute and enforce the Act and subsequent Orders through the police and to appoint Inspectors.

In 1905 Stewart Stockman became Chief Veterinary Officer and greatly extended the Board's veterinary laboratory services, believing wholeheartedly in the importance of research being undertaken into the nature of disease before the adoption of measures for its control. Alperton Lodge was taken over for use as a laboratory in 1908 and, among other work, began production of anti-swine fever serum in 1914 because imported supplies had been cut off due to the war. That same year, with a grant from the Development Commissioners, a new

65. One of the many monuments raised in remembrance of the Cattle Plague of 1865–67

Central Veterinary Laboratory was under construction at Weybridge, and was completed in 1917. It contained five laboratories, offices, and a building for the continued production of serum. In the 1920s the laboratory was chiefly concerned with the diagnosis of scheduled diseases, research on foot-and-mouth disease and work on poultry. The outbreak of war meant that the laboratory was again called on to undertake an urgent anthrax vaccine and anti-serum production programme. A reserve of 2 million doses of vaccine, renewable every six months, was rapidly built up and distributed throughout the country. A milestone in laboratory history was provided by the employment of female labour for the first time to help in this work.

In the postwar period the Central Veterinary Laboratory continued to expand – from five to 13 departments, including the Lasswade Laboratory at Edinburgh and the Cattle Breeding Centre at Reading. At the same time its responsibilities were widened to include development of new tests for the diagnosis of diseases. In this connection pioneer work at CVL led to the automation of the testing of blood samples collected for the brucellosis eradication campaign and, later, the eradication of Aujezky's disease in pigs.

Routine surveillance disease monitoring and the early detection and control, by eradication or other method, of new diseases are a major part of the State Veterinary Service's work. A computerised veterinary investigation diagnosis analysis (VIDA) and the Zoonoses Order Data System have been established and in 1972 an Epidemiology Unit was set up. The Cattle Breeding Centre at Reading provides a commercial artificial insemination service for cattle and pigs.

A landmark in 1934 was the recommendation of the Economic Advisory Committee on Cattle Diseases for obligatory routine veterinary inspection of herds and dairies, expansion of the veterinary service and tuberculin testing.

The Agriculture Act 1937 amalgamated all the veterinary services (the Inspectors in MAF, veterinary officers in the Department of Agriculture for Scotland and local authority inspectors) into one national veterinary service, and the actual transfer took place in April 1938. MAF was simultaneously given additional responsibilities for the diagnosis, prevention and eradication of diseases of economic importance.

The Veterinary Investigation Service celebrated its 60th anniversary in 1982. Although agricultural colleges and departments in universities had given advice to farmers before World War One, the first Veterinary Advisory Officer was not appointed until 1922 – at Cardiff, followed soon after by posts at Newcastle, Bangor and Sutton Bonington. By the end of World War Two there were 13 officers, all but one at agricultural education establishments. Now known as Senior Veterinary Investigation Officers, they carried out diagnostic work on diseases of cattle, sheep and pigs, and research on poultry diseases. In 1946 the service was brought into the Animal Health division of MAF and formed a link between the Central Veterinary Laboratory and the field staffs. Thereafter the Service's work expanded greatly, and in 1958 the Animal Health divisions were reorganised, largely on a regional basis. In 1971 the field and investigation sides of the division were integrated and the whole Veterinary Service incorporated within ADAS.

Although most of their business continues to be diagnostic, other functions include monitoring the state of animal disease in local areas, *ad hoc* research on local problems, carrying out surveys of disease incidence and collaborating in field trials of new methods of disease control. ADAS provides advice for livestock producers that ranges from questions of breeding to meeting changing market demands, while a network of laboratories and veterinary investigation centres can give on-call problem-solving and diagnostic services. The country is now free of many pests and diseases. Measures have been taken to eradicate sheep scab and warble fly, and there are strict controls over the importation of animals, meat and meat products.

The SVS is responsible for animal welfare on farms and for monitoring compliance with the animal welfare codes of practice covering cattle, sheep, goats, pigs, poultry, rabbits and deer. The welfare of livestock in markets, slaughterhouses, during transport, export and import, is also an issue of major concern and a responsibility shared with local authorities.

The SVS's objective remains the same – to contribute to improvements in animal and public health by providing a diagnostic, advisory and consultative service, support for statutory and health schemes, for R & D and for educational facilities.

# THE LAND

*THE RURAL SCENE HAS BEEN
CHANGING SINCE FARMING
BEGAN AND FARMING USES
OVER THREE-QUARTERS OF
BRITAIN'S LAND AREA.*

*Farming UK*, HMSO, 1987

The oldest functions of the Ministry are those concerned with land on the one hand and animal diseases on the other. The Land Commission for England (1882) had formerly looked after three aspects of land tenure (the commutation of tithes, enclosures and the enfranchisement of copyhold land) which, in its turn, the newly-formed Board of Agriculture took over when it subsumed the Land Commission in 1889. Extra Commissioners were employed for work on small holdings and allotments, and between the wars they dealt as well with tithe apportionment, reported on agricultural conditions and rent movements, and undertook valuations and land transactions on behalf of the Ministry. They were key figures in setting up the County War Agricultural Executive Committees, and acted as go-betweens with the Minister.

In the reorganisation following the war, the Agricultural Land Service was created under the Agriculture Act 1947 from a nucleus of officers from the Land Commission Service and from qualified land agents and auctioneers, surveyors and estate agents to complement the Land Commissioners. This took effect in 1948 and staff carried out land agency duties and advised on farm buildings. During the war the War Ags had requisitioned land, and rents had to be agreed and arrangements made to return the land to its former owners. Some land was bought by the Ministry, and the Agricultural Land Commission was set up, also in 1948, to advise on this and to manage the land. A small group of economists, geographers and geologists researched land use matters and developed the Agricultural Land Classification System. The Town & Country Planning Act 1947 had given county councils the task of preparing development plans and town maps, and the Land Service offered guidance on agricultural matters

*66. Poster from the United Committee for Taxation of Land Values, 1910*

64

and on day-to-day aspects of individual applications, and were sometimes involved as expert witnesses at public enquiries.

By the end of the 1950s most requisitioned land had been returned to its owners and post-war supervisory powers had been repealed. But there was still a need for increased food production, and the Farm Improvements Scheme, authorised under the 1957 Agriculture Act, was the first comprehensive measure designed to increase farming efficiency by giving grants towards the cost of capital equipment and for long-term improvements. The Land Service helped farmers with the technical aspects of proposals. In 1957, following the recommendations of the Arton Wilson Committee, the administrative work carried out in the county offices was given a separate substantive status in its own right, which led to the establishment of the current Divisional Executive Officer posts.

Advisory work grew more important and the Land Service took part in farm demonstrations and exhibitions. In 1971 the Service became part of ADAS and when the UK joined the Common Market, EC directives widened the scope of the Farm Capital Grants Scheme. Five-year development plans were the primary responsibility of local District Agriculture Advisers, and enabled a whole-farm approach to be taken to improvement.

## SMALL HOLDINGS

The Small Holdings Act 1892 authorised county councils to acquire land to provide holdings for sale or to let. The Act was unpopular, and it was 16 years before another attempt was made to, as they said, 'colonise our own country' with a further consolidating Act in 1908. Two more Acts were passed during World War One which empowered the Board of Agriculture to acquire land for establishing experimental colonies for ex-servicemen. The provision of small holdings had been looked on as part of a social policy of maintaining the rural population, of resettling ex-servicemen, and in the years of depression between the two wars, of settling unemployed workers on the land. In 1934 the Land Settlement Association was set up by government to 'carry out an experimental scheme for the provision of smallholdings for unemployed persons . . . and to act as agent for the Commissioner for the Special Areas.' After the outbreak of war many of the original

67. A satisfied customer

settlers returned to the towns and were replaced by experienced agricultural workers.

Earlier legislation was replaced by part IV of the Agriculture Act 1947 under which small holdings were to be provided to give those with experience an opportunity of becoming farmers on their own account. County councils were obliged to provide holdings, acquire land and look after equipment, and Ministers could also acquire or designate land and make loans to tenants for working capital. The Land Settlement Association's estates were transferred to the Minister and the Association became his agent for those estates.

After enactment of the 1970 Agriculture Act, county councils no longer had to provide holdings on demand, although they could rent them out and were allowed to make or guarantee loans for working capital. In 1985 the Land Settlement Association was wound up, and currently local authorities provide over six thousand statutory small holdings in England and something under 1,000 in Wales for experienced people, and make loans of up to 75% of required working capital to their tenants.

Responsibility for allotments was taken over by the Board of Agriculture from the Local Government Board in 1908. They were originally intended for the 'labouring population' but their popularity received a big boost in World War One, and an even bigger one in World War Two, with the 'Dig for Victory' campaign. Between

# Allotments.

On Monday we had Beans and Swedes,
  On Tuesday Swedes and Beans,
On Wednesday we had Haricots
  And some Swedes instead of greens.

On Thursday we had Beans again
  With just a little soup
Made from some Swedes and Haricots,
  But we called it "Cereal Soup."

On Friday just by way of a change
  We had Swedes fried in slices,
And finished up with Butter Beans
  Instead of nice cool ices.

On Saturday we've Swedes mashed up,
  And there's Beans again for Sunday,
But we quite expect to have a change
  From Beans to Swedes next Monday.

*68. 'City dwellers by hundreds and thousands rediscovered the thrill and wonder of making things grow.'*

1939–1945 the number of allotments rose to over 1,400,000 and produced 2½–3 million tons of food. Numbers have fallen somewhat since those days. These days the primary duty of providing allotments belongs to local authorities and the permission of the Department of the Environment is needed for any change of land use.

## LAXTON

Laxton in Nottinghamshire is the last existing open field village in England. It comprises about 1,830 acres divided into 15 farms and six small holdings. It was offered to MAF in 1952 and is the only surviving village to have open fields cultivated in the way common in the Middle Ages. The system is administered by the Court Leet of the Manor (consisting of all the occupiers of the land) and until 1981 the Minister of Agriculture was Lord of the Manor. Laxton was taken over by the Ministry with the intention of keeping it as a working example and was handed to the Agricultural Land Commission 'to preserve the open fields, to help [its] tenants to meet the demands of the future'.

The Laxton Estate was sold to the Crown Estate Commissioners in 1981 for £1 million, on the undertaking that they would continue the open field system and associated customs. A three-year programme of rotation is followed, with winter corn/spring corn, beans or clover/ and a fallow field. Laxton was designated a Conservation Area in 1972.

## LAND DRAINAGE

For about 150 years the Ministry and its predecessors have had to administer acts concerned with the efficient drainage of land. The first Land Drainage Act was passed in 1846 and authorised the issue of loans from public funds to enable landlords to carry out schemes approved by the Enclosure Commissioners. Later acts provided for loans from private sources. The Land Drainage Act of 1930, based on the report of a Royal Commission, rationalised the law and created Catchment Boards with powers of enforcement for whole watershed areas of rivers. The River Boards Act 1948 carried the process a stage further by providing for the establishment of river boards

*69. Thames Flood Barrier*

for England and Wales, and the 1976 Land Drainage Act consolidated the law and empowered water authorities to exercise general supervision over land drainage matters, with regional committees exercising most of these functions.

The Ministry gives grants for draining farm land, combined with advice to landowners and farmers on drainage. A field drainage experimental unit was set up in Cambridge by MAFF's Land Drainage & Machinery division in 1963 to carry out research and give advice on the performance of different drainage systems such as the trenchless method, the use of plastic pipes and the mole drainage technique of draining clay soils. MAFF also oversees the work of the authorities responsible for arterial drainage and sea defences. During and after World War Two, the Ministry and County Committees operated a service for draining private land on a repayment basis and for restoring land worked for opencast coal.

The water authorities are now responsible for the water reaching the sea, as well as for coastal defence. Some members are appointed by MAFF, and the Ministry can give grants towards improvements and for new works. The water authorities also protect low-lying land from flooding, from the open sea or from tidal action in estuaries. When widespread flooding occurred, as in the floods of 1947, 1953 and 1960, it was the Ministry that co-ordinated emergency help. For example, in January 1953, a combination of strong winds and high tides along the east coast caused the loss of 300 lives, damage estimated at over £40 million and 160,000 acres of flooded land. Although the River Boards repaired the breaches and reconstructed the sea defences, the Ministry had to ensure that the work was done as soon as possible, and that flooded land was quickly brought back into production. Troops – 14,000 of them – worked on emergency repairs until civilian contractors took over, and MAF engineers were sent in as reinforcements.

The Thames Tidal Flood Prevention Scheme, opened by the Queen in 1984, is the largest flood defence project ever undertaken in Britain and cost over £750 million, financed to a large extent by MAFF grants. The threat of flooding from the sea has always been with Londoners, and record high tides have often affected the city in the past. In 1953 London had narrowly escaped the east coast floods and a Committee appointed that year recommended that the feasibility of a movable barrier to close the Thames against dangerously high tides should be investigated. Another recommendation led to the creation of a flood warning service for the east coast, including the Thames, operated from the Meteorological Office, but administered by MAF. From 1956 into the 60s, engineers examined the question of a barrier and advised that it could be built but only at huge cost. A 1967 review concluded that the risk must not be allowed to continue and that a barrier above Long Reach would be the most economical defence.

Several working parties were set up and ministerial approval given to the scheme in December 1970. In 1972 the Greater London Council was given specific powers under the Thames Barrier & Flood Prevention Act to build a barrier at Woolwich. MAFF staff appraised the proposed works, liaised with the local authorities and their consulting engineers to establish design criteria, approved contracts and monitored progress. After much delay, the barrier first closed on 31 October 1982 at low water, and in February 1983 it was shut for the first time in response to a flood warning.

# THE NATIONAL STUD

*THIS QUESTION OF THE PRODUCTION AND MAINTENANCE IN GREAT BRITAIN OF AN AMPLE SUPPLY OF LIGHT HORSES OF SUITABLE STAMP...*

Committee on the Supply of Horses for Military Purposes, *Report* Cd 8134, HMSO, 1915

The National Stud came into being in 1916 when Colonel Hall Walker, later Lord Wavertree, offered all his bloodstock to the nation on condition that the Government bought his breeding establishment at Tully, Co. Kildare. This included 43 mares from some of the best lines in the British Isles (The Stud had produced Derby and 2,000 Guineas winner *Minoru*, Oaks winner *Cherry Lass*, St. Leger winner *Night Hawk*, and many other top-class thoroughbreds). The value of the gift amounted to over £80,000 at pre-war prices, and it was accepted on the understanding that maintenance of first-class stock would ensure breeding of high quality light horses for the Army. From the start, the Stud was placed under the control of the Board of Agriculture.

Its original role diminished with the increasing mechanisation of the Army, but the Government continued to operate it on commercial lines, selling most of the progeny as yearlings at auction at prices up to 18,000 guineas, and retaining some fillies for future breeding. This proved very successful and the Stud bred many classic winners. It remained in Ireland until 1943 when the Tully property was handed over to the Irish Government under the Irish Treaty. The bloodstock was transferred to Sandley Stud in Dorset, and after World War Two, its facilities were expanded by the acquisition of a stud at West Grinstead in Sussex.

Policy was reviewed in the mid-1950s by a Committee under Sir Percy Loraine, which recommended that the Stud should keep high-quality stallions available for private breeders and continue to maintain an establishment of breeding mares representative of some of the best blood lines. The purchase and sale of bloodstock other than yearlings and foals was carried out by the Ministry, advised by a small expert Committee, and racehorses were leased (in return for half their net winnings) to the Queen, who defrayed all the expenses of maintaining them during their

70. Mill Reef *by* Never Bend *out of* Milan Mill, *who stood at the National Stud from 1973–1986 and was Europe's leading sire in 1978 and 1987*

racing life. The cost of the Stud was borne on the MAFF Vote, and all receipts paid into the Exchequer.

The Stud had many very successful winners, notable names being *Blandford*, sire of four Derby winners, *Big Game*, who went to the Stud in 1943 and by 1961 had sired winners of 395 races, and *Sun Chariot*, bred at the Stud, whose progeny included eight Classics winners.

There was a radical change of policy in 1963, when it was decided to sell the mares and concentrate exclusively on the standing high-class stallions. The two existing studs were sold and a new purpose-designed Stud built on 500 acres of land at Newmarket, leased from the Jockey Club. In the same year responsibility for the Stud was transferred to the Horserace Betting Levy Board, and in 1986 a new Board of Management was appointed to secure a viable future for the Stud and to run it as a centre of excellence.

# ORDNANCE SURVEY

*EVERY PRINCE SHOULD HAVE...*
*A DRAUGHT OF HIS COUNTRY*
*AND DESTINATIONS TO SEE*
*HOW THE GROUND LIES... SUCH*
*A MAP OR SURVEY WOULD BE*
*USEFUL BOTH IN TIME OF WAR*
*AND PEACE.*

Thomas Burnet.
*The theory of the earth, 1684*

The newly-established Board of Agriculture took over responsibility for the Ordnance Survey from the Commissioners of Works and Public Buildings on 1st April 1890, and the President assumed the powers possessed until 1855 by the Master General of the Ordnance. The appointment of Sir George Leach as Permanent Secretary to the Board was encouraging, as he was 'perfectly conversant with the work of the department' and was able to appreciate proposals made for improving the Survey's work.

The Ordnance Survey had been established in 1791 under the Board of Ordnance because of the military need for accurate maps when the country was under threat of invasion from France. Its original task was a survey of the whole country on a scale of 1″ to the mile, changed in 1858 by the recommendations of a Royal Commission to a scale of 1/2500, apart from mountain and moorland areas. The first 1″ sheet covered Kent in 1801, and by 1840 the country was mapped at that scale as far north as Hull and Preston. Such a survey was needed to provide reliable, large-scale plans both for planning and for transfer of land because of the rapid growth of building and of the railway system following the Industrial Revolution. All the smaller scale maps were derived from the original survey which was completed in 1895, and has been regularly revised since then.

The Ordnance Survey stayed under military control until 1870 when it became responsible to the Board of Works. It had military obligations to train soldiers in surveying, and many of its staff served with the forces in time of war. In World War One its duties included the preparation of nearly 33 million maps, plans and diagrams for the Army and Navy. The Ordnance Survey prepared plans for sites for fortifications and munition works, and fixed positions of coastal defence guns. MAF was responsible for pay, allowances, rations, quarters, travelling, medical expenses and training costs for serving officers on the Ordnance Survey. In World War Two the Survey helped to prepare around 120 million maps for the invasion of Normandy, and produced maps and surveys for the war effort, mainly concerned with the mapping of foreign countries, but some connected with the defence of Great Britain.

After the war, the staff began to resurvey all the major towns in Great Britain on a scale of about 50″ to the mile, and to revise the old 25″ series for the rest of the country. From 1938 onwards, when an Establishment & Finance Officer was first appointed, directors of the Ordnance Survey were largely autonomous, and had their own Parliamentary Vote. This degree of independence was endorsed by the Estimates Committee in 1963, although the Ordnance Survey still remained under the Department broadly responsible for 'holding the Government's corpus of knowledge on land'. In January 1965, its transfer to the Ministry of Land & Natural Resources was debated, while an officer of MAFF wrote that the 'present arrangements work well; there seems to be little point in disturbing them . . .' However, the Ordnance Survey went to MLNR in that year, and in February 1967, responsibility for the Department was transferred to the Ministry of Housing and Local Government.

# 7 FLOWERS, FRUIT AND VEGETABLES

## HORTICULTURE

*THIS OUR EARTH PRODUCES
NOT ONLY A SUFFICIENCY AND
A SUPERABUNDANCE, BUT IN
ONE YEAR POURS A
CORNUCOPIA OF GOOD THINGS
FORTH, ENOUGH TO FILL US ALL
FOR MANY YEARS IN
SUCCESSION.*

Jefferies, R.
*The story of my heart*, 1883

The Board of Agriculture Act 1889 included horticulture in its provisions but for many years no particular attention was paid to the special needs of flower, fruit and vegetable growers. The Board had powers concerning the cultivation of horticultural crops in the open and under glass, it inspected and certificated crops for export and gave technical advice on insects, fungi, pests and diseases. World War One, however, was the turning point for this sector of the agricultural industry. The growth of the allotment movement underlined the usefulness of intensive cultivation and because the Board of Agriculture was responsible for small holdings it had to look after the needs of small producers.

One of the handicaps to the sale of home produce was that there were no recognised sizes for containers. The Ministry drew up a scheme for standardising packages which was submitted to and approved by the trade. Packages of a standard cubic capacity were stamped as approved by the Ministry, beginning with chip baskets for strawberries, and a number of demonstrations of methods of grading and packing were held in different parts of the country. In 1924 MAF established an experimental apple picking station in Cambridgeshire. Local growers were invited to bring their fruit to be graded and packed by Ministry staff, and the station was subsequently taken over by a local association of growers.

After World War One commercial fruit growing was badly organised, with new cultivars being introduced haphazardly and orchards containing a mixture of good, bad and indifferent cultivars. Some of the major fruit growers decided that the whole system needed rationalising and that a testing station should be set up where new and standard fruits could be grown and studied. In

*71. Spraying fruit trees, 1933*

October 1922 the Ministry and the Royal Horticultural Society formed a committee to discuss the establishment of the National Fruit Trials at the RHS gardens at Wisley. All the hardy fruits were tested for merit and as well, collections of fruits were grown as a 'living reference library'. Originally the RHS provided the land, collections, labour and expertise, and the Ministry gave a grant which diminished as the Trials began to prosper, and finally ceased in 1943. In 1946 the Trials were placed under the aegis of the newly-formed National Agricultural Advisory Service (NAAS). A more spacious site in a fruit-growing area was found and the move to Brogdale Experimental

Horticultural Station near Faversham in Kent started in 1952 and was completed by 1960. *The National Apple Register of the UK* was compiled at Brogdale and published in 1971, and is a standard reference work to this day, consisting of a factual history of apple cultivars known to be grown in Great Britain from 1853 to 1968.

The National Fruit Trials is the international registration authority for apples and the national registration authority for all hardy fruits, while the large collections of cultivars at Brogdale also serve as gene banks for plant breeders and as a workshop for scientists. The apple collection contains over 2,000 varieties and there are also collections of cherries, pears, plums, black and red currants and gooseberries. New varieties and seedlings are sent to Brogdale from breeders in the UK and abroad, and are tested for their commercial potential. A range of trials examine the techniques of production and crop yields of certain fruits.

Quality standards for apples, pears, tomatoes, cucumbers and cauliflowers were introduced at the wholesale point of sale under the 1964 Agricultural & Horticultural Act. The intention was to help home growers compete with imports, and a Horticultural Marketing Inspectorate was set up to enforce the regulations. Their work was widened to include mandatory grading when Britain acceded to the European Community, and they worked in wholesale markets, ports and docks, airports and depots. Inspectors advise on quality, labelling and packing, demonstrations are held at conferences and at experimental horticulture stations, and the Inspectorate keeps in touch with all sections of the industry and trade.

Price guarantees under the 1947 and 1957 Agriculture Acts did not extend to horticultural produce, which is much more perishable and variable in quality than farm produce. At that period successive governments gave protection by tariffs to the home producer during his main marketing season without impeding imports when they were needed. But problems of glut and wastage were unavoidable, and worries as to how the marketing system might be improved led to the appointment of the Runciman Committee on Horticultural Marketing in 1955. Its report investigated facilities and methods of marketing home-produced and imported vegetables, fruit and flowers, and possible improvements in distribution. The Government responded two years later, agreeing that

72. *Horticulturalists at work*

the marketing system was generally satisfactory but could be improved in details. It set up a Horticultural Marketing Council in 1960, consisting of 28 members appointed by Ministers, and representatives of the producers, importers, wholesalers, retailers and horticultural workers. Its functions included obtaining and disseminating information about supply, demand and prices; promoting research; formulating standards, certifying produce and registering trade marks. From May 1960–1963 the Council was financed by the Treasury and produced several reports on different aspects of marketing but it expired in 1963 when the Treasury grant was withdrawn and the industry failed to give sufficient support to its subscription scheme to keep it going.

In addition to its responsibilities under the Agricultural Marketing Acts, the Ministry encouraged voluntary co-operation among producers. The Central Council for Agricultural and Horticultural Co-operation was established under the 1967 Agriculture Act, with the dual role of developing co-operation among producers and of operating a grant scheme for co-operative activities. In 1974 the Council was made responsible for improving agricultural marketing. It was dissolved in March 1983 and

*73. Old Covent Garden market*

its work transferred to a new organisation – Food from Britain.

The Apple and Pear Development Council also began life in 1967, with members appointed by the Minister and including growers, employees and specialists. Its aim was to increase consumption of English fruit by promoting production and marketing, through research, publicity and co-operation. A more recent body is the Horticultural Development Council, set up in July 1986, which funds research and development by means of a compulsory levy on growers. The Council keeps a register of growers, collects information and statistical returns, and its remit covers all horticultural crops except apples, pears and hops.

## BEES

Bees have a significant role to play in UK horticulture because they make a valuable contribution to pollination and provide part-time occupation for thousands of people. MAFF helps beekeepers maintain a healthy honeybee population and administers a licensing system to control imports and minimise the risk of disease. The National Beekeeping Unit at Luddington Experimental Horticultural Station in Warwickshire has about 200 colonies of bees and gives practical advice on all aspects of apiary management including honey and pollen production, queen rearing, disease control, and methods of feeding for optimal colony development.

Beekeeping seminars covering established practices as well as new developments are held regularly at Luddington, and unit staff also pass on information in leaflets, lectures and articles in specialist journals. An important aspect of the Unit's work is the diagnosis of serious diseases of bees from samples of bees, comb and hive debris sent in from all parts of England and Wales under the provisions of the Bees Act 1980 by beekeepers and by Ministry Bees Officers, appointed to examine hives under the Bee Diseases Control Order 1982. ADAS now charges for all its beekeeping services other than those relating to statutory diseases of bees.

## MARKETS

Wholesale markets also come within the remit of the Minister. Markets themselves were often set up long ago in the middle of big cities, with the result that they became congested, with little room for movement of produce and unsatisfactory conditions for buyers and sellers. There were five markets in London alone: Covent Garden, Spitalfields, Bow, Brentford and Stratford, and a smaller one at Greenwich. Under the Agricultural & Horticultural Act 1964 grants were made available for the rebuilding of wholesale horticultural markets, and major centres such as those at Bristol, Cardiff, Birmingham, Manchester, Leeds and Liverpool, as well as the London markets received substantial help through grant aid.

Many of the largest markets have now moved away, typical examples being Billingsgate Fish Market and Covent Garden. The right to hold a market at Covent Garden was originally granted by Royal Charter in 1670 to the Earl of Bedford, and a 1928 Act provided for the reorganisation of the site and prescribed how it should be laid out and used. The Runciman Committee Report of 1957 on Horticultural Marketing looked at the problems of markets and recommended the establishment of a public authority to reorganise Covent Garden. A Market Authority was created by statute in 1961 to provide facilities for dealing with bulk horticultural produce, storage and parking space; its members were appointed by MAFF and the Charter extinguished. A further Act in 1966 provided for the transfer of Covent Garden Market to a site at Nine Elms and during 1974 the market moved there from its old location.

*74. Toll board at market, 1911*

# PLANTS AND SEEDS

Legislation on aspects of plant health has been in force for well over a century. In 1889 the new Board of Agriculture inherited the duties of the Privy Council under the Destructive Insects Act 1877, a piece of legislation that had been enacted to prevent the introduction into this country of the Colorado Beetle, which was then attacking the potato crop in the USA and Canada. That same year a solitary beetle was found at Liverpool Docks on a ship carrying Texan wheat and this prompted Britain to introduce its first plant health legislation, referring only to Colorado beetle. The first warning leaflet for farmers was issued in the *Journal of the Board of Agriculture* in September 1901.

The Destructive Insects and Pests Act 1907 extended the 1877 Act to cover all insects, fungi and other destructive plant pests, and in 1927 the existing powers were again expanded to cover bacteria and other vegetable or animal organisms and to make new provisions for compensation for crops removed or destroyed. These three Acts were consolidated in the Plant Health Act 1967, which remains the basic plant health legislation in Great Britain today, although amended by the European Communities Act 1972.

Many early orders made under the Destructive Insects and Pests Acts related to pests and diseases of potatoes. Potato Wart Disease was widespread in the early years of this century, but outbreaks are now fairly rare due to statutory measures and the development of immune varieties. The battle to prevent Colorado beetle from becoming established here has been waged successfully throughout the century, with eradication of outbreaks in 1901, the 1930s and during World War Two. No further colonies were discovered until 1976 and 1977. The beetle

*75. MAFF publicity poster*

is very distinctive and has been used to good effect in MAFF publicity to alert the public to locate any insects gaining entry before they reach their host plants. It has been estimated that if the beetle did establish itself in the UK it would cost growers about £5 million annually in lost yields and pesticide treatments.

Orders have also been made under the primary legislation to cover a range of other serious plant pests and diseases and over the years have laid down specific conditions under which plants and plant products may be imported. Since accession to the European Communities, MAFF has implemented Community rules on plant health matters. The Plant Health and Seeds Inspectorate is MAFF's 'front line' for dealing with statutory pests and diseases; until April 1987 the Inspectorate, ADAS's Harpenden Laboratory and the Plant Health division were a triumvirate, but now the Inspectorate comes directly under the Plant Health division. ADAS Scientific Staff provide technical back-up and, through a network of plant clinics, give landowners, farmers and local authorities information and advice on pest and disease problems. The voluntary code on pesticides has now been superseded by statutory controls over their supply and use introduced in the Food & Environment Protection Act 1985.

ADAS's Aerial Photography Unit, based at the Cambridge regional office, carries out surveys to pinpoint where to look for suspected plant disease, and also undertakes contract work for local authorities. It owns one plane and uses experts to interpret what is seen and photographed from the air.

## PLANT BREEDERS' RIGHTS
In the mid-1950s the Committee on Transactions in Seeds, which had been considering the reorganisation of seed law, was asked to assess the case for introducing a system of protection for new varieties of plants, somewhat on the lines of those already existing for protection of written works and inventions. The Committee's second report in 1960 recommended that a Plant Breeders' Rights (PBR) system should be introduced by statute and in 1965 the current arrangements were laid down under Part 1 of the Plant Varieties and Seeds Act 1964 which established the Plant Variety Rights Office under a Controller. The Office is in Cambridge, near the National Institute of Agricultural Botany building.

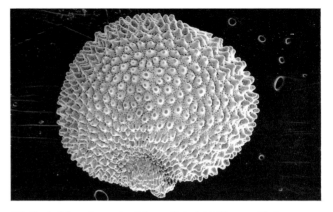

76. *Seed of the red campion (*silene dioica*) highly magnified*

Although somewhat similar to patents, PBR differ in several respects mainly because they are concerned with living plant material. Since a plant can reproduce itself rapidly, a new variety is open to unauthorised exploitation, so any protection system must be capable of identifying it clearly and controlling its reproduction. In the UK such control is vested by law in the plant breeder. Before a plant can be registered in the Plant Variety Rights Office, growing trials are carried out to ensure that the variety is 'distinct, uniform and stable'; PBR is granted for a period of 20–30 years, allowing the breeder to control through licence the reproduction of his protected variety for sale, and the sale of seed or other propagating material.

PBR also gives the holder exclusive rights in the registered name of his variety. Guidelines for plant nomenclature have been laid down by the International Union for the Protection of New Varieties of Plants to ensure that each variety is given a distinctive name. This name must be used by anyone selling seed of the variety, and must not be used when selling seed of another variety of the same species.

The introduction of PBR has encouraged commercial plant breeding during the last two decades, the number of companies involved has increased considerably, and private sector investment has risen. The number of new plant varieties has also increased, and disease-resistant varieties have been produced.

SEEDS

The earliest legislation on seeds was the Adulteration of Seeds Act 1869 which made it an offence to sell in the UK any killed or dyed seeds. Similar regulations were in force by 1914 in most of Europe, the United States and several British dominions. In 1900 the Board of Agriculture set up a departmental committee to inquire into the conditions of sale in agricultural seeds. This recommended the establishment of a seed testing station to help farmers, and the first official testing station in the UK was set up that same year in Ireland, with another established in Scotland in 1914. Demand for increased food production during World War One led to moves to increase seed supply and to establish an official seed testing station in England – first in London in 1917, but transferred to Cambridge in 1921. The first regulations made under the 1920 Seeds Act came into force in 1922 and stipulated that the purchaser should be given a true description of the seed at time of sale.

By 1954 it was obvious that wider powers were needed than those provided by the 1920 Act. The Committee on Transactions in Seeds was appointed to examine the workings of the Act, the contractual relationship between buyers and sellers of seed, and measures of seed control. Its first report appeared in November 1957 and its second, dealing with PBR in July 1960. The Committee's recommendations were implemented by regulations made in 1961 and the Plant Varieties & Seeds Act 1964 provided for performance trials and for the setting up of an index of names of plant varieties. This enabling act is the main legislation regulating seeds and plant variety matters in the UK. In due course the Act was amended by schedule 4D of the European Communities Act 1972 so that EC seeds directives could be implemented.

Certification became compulsory for most varieties under EC directives, and many more people were needed to carry out inspection, sampling and testing. These tasks were carried out under licence on the understanding that licensees would be subject to official supervision by the Agricultural Departments. Day-to-day technical operation of the seed certification schemes is carried out for MAFF by the Seed Production branch of the National Institute of Agricultural Botany. There are three official testing stations in the UK, based at Cambridge, Edinburgh and Belfast, and a common seeds regime operates throughout the Community.

# ROYAL BOTANIC GARDENS, KEW

GOD ALMIGHTY FIRST PLANTED
A GARDEN; AND, INDEED, IT IS
THE PUREST OF HUMAN
PLEASURES.

Francis Bacon. *Of gardens*

Kew Gardens first came under the control of the Board of Agriculture in 1903, because of the direct relevance to the Board of its research and educational work. The original 9-acre botanic garden at Kew was initiated by Princess Augusta in 1759, in the grounds of her home at Kew House. When she died in 1772, her son King George III united the gardens with those of Richmond Lodge, and appointed Sir Joseph Banks as botanical adviser. Banks had just returned from Captain Cook's first expedition to Australia; he enhanced the fine collections at Kew by dispatching plant collectors to newly discovered regions. For example, in 1775 Francis Masson brought back from southern Africa the specimen of *Encephalantos longifolius* which is still growing at Kew, and new species of heathers (*Erica*). Within a few years, the Royal Gardens at Kew were internationally renowned for their collections of exotic and useful plants.

After the death of George III, and of Banks in 1820, Kew was somewhat neglected, and there was much public criticism by the time Queen Victoria came to the throne. A House of Commons Committee was appointed in 1837, under the chairmanship of John Lindley, to look into the management of the Royal Gardens at Kew, Windsor and Kensington; their report drew attention to the benefits of a central, well-equipped botanic garden, its uses for medicine, horticulture, manufacturers and 'the economic development of the colonies'. The gardens at Kew were subsequently transferred from the charge of the Lord Steward of the Royal Household and put under the control of the Commissioners of Woods, Forests, Land Resources, Works & Buildings in 1840, and Sir William Hooker FRS was appointed as Director in 1841.

There followed years of intense development in re-

77. *Group of gardeners, Royal Botanic Gardens Kew, c. 1900*

sponse to ever-growing demands from Government, industry, the colonies and the general public. People loved the new Museums of Economic Botany (opened in 1848), the Palm House (also 1848), and the Temperate House (1862). They flocked to Kew in increasing numbers, reaching a peak of over two million visitors in 1903. The number of scientific visitors and the amount of corres-

*78. Main gates, Kew, designed by Decimus Burton in 1848*

pondence also grew because of the excellence of the collections in the gardens, the Herbarium (1853) and the Library, both based on the fine collections of Hooker and George Bentham. Hooker received well over 35,500 letters on scientific matters, which are now in Kew's archives.

Plant explorers continued to be sent out, and included the Director's son Joseph, who went to Australia and the Antarctic on the *Erebus* and *Terror* expeditions in 1839–43 and to the Himalayas in 1847–51. When Sir William Hooker died in 1865, the Royal Gardens at Kew were pre-eminent among the world's botanic gardens and to this day Kew is seen as a model for new botanical institutes the world over.

Sir Joseph Hooker succeeded his father as Director and established procedures and relationships with Government and industry that served Kew well long after his retirement. Improvements in the collections and in government organisation made it feasible to prepare more accurate descriptions of the plant resources of the British colonies, for example, the *Flora of British India* and the *Flora of Tropical Africa*. The richness of the Library at Kew made it possible to compile *Index Kewensis* with money provided by Charles Darwin, an old friend of Sir Joseph Hooker. The *Index Kewensis* is a listing of given Latin names of plants, citing the publication when the name was first used and the plant described; it is still compiled, and contains about $1\frac{1}{4}$ million names.

*79. The Temperate House, designed by Decimus Burton*

Particular attention was given to the economic development of the colonies, and the Director of Kew liaised directly with the Foreign Office, the Colonial Office and the India Office. Horticultural staff were trained for work overseas, experimental stations were set up in various countries, and potentially useful crops propagated and distributed. In this way the rubber industry in the Far East was developed and malaria controlled in India by quinine, produced from the South American Cinchona plant.

In 1876, a new laboratory was set up for research into plant anatomy, physiology and chemistry, with funds provided by Mr T J Philips-Jodrell. It rapidly attracted many distinguished scientists, including C F Cross, E J Bevan and C Beadle, whose fundamental work on the

80. *Moving palms at Kew*

lignin chemistry led to the development of the rayon industry. From its earliest days, the Jodrell Laboratory has tested and identified samples of economic plant products, archaeological and forensic materials, and undertaken major research projects culminating in the volumes on *The Anatomy of the Dicotyledons*, *The Anatomy of the Monocotyledons* and, more recently, tree root analysis. The Jodrell Laboratory also has active research programmes in cytology and in the chemistry and biochemistry of medicine and anti-insect compounds from plants.

In 1914, a plant pathology unit was established at Kew, which in 1920 moved to Harpenden to be nearer the Rothamsted Experimental Station; that unit is now part of MAFF. Kew's interest in tropical economic botany led, after World War Two, to the development of an Intermediate Quarantine Service for bananas, whereby plants intended for a third country were kept at Kew for a full season of growth under careful surveillance, to ensure that they carried no disease to the receiving country. This was vital in building up the collections of bananas in Trinidad, for example. The service (funded by the Colonial Office and ODA) was expanded to include sugar cane and cocoa, but ceased in 1984 when funding stopped. Kew has long assisted MAFF, Customs & Excise and other Departments in the identification of plant imports and exports, and of plant hosts of insect and other pests.

World War Two was a strange time at Kew. Most of the collections were dispersed for safety, and staff were much involved in war work, advising on botanical sources of medicines, vitamins and alternative sources of vital commodities such as rubber (from dandelions, and salsify from Russia), paper, and plywood. In collaboration with other organisations, Kew produced rosehip syrup and developed a palatable marmalade from green walnuts. Crops of belladonna, colchicum and digitalis were grown to ease wartime drug scarcities. Half of Kew Green was dug up for vegetable production, and a MAF demonstration model allotment was maintained, designed to keep a family of four in vegetables for most of the year. Plots were laid out to produce seed and some plant houses given over to tomatoes.

In the late 1950s, the work and organisation of Kew was reviewed, and a renewal began which is still in progress today. The Bicentenary in 1959 was marked by a visit from HM the Queen; she returned in 1969 to open the new wing of the Herbarium containing the Library, and again in 1982 to reopen the Temperate House. A new building replaced the old Jodrell Laboratory, work on plant genetics began, and seed banks with associated research programmes were set up to store viable seed for research and conservation, in conjunction with the UN International Board for Plant Genetic Resources. The International Union for the Conservation of Nature based their Threatened Plants Committee at Kew, and in 1975 Kew was designated as the scientific authority for the UK Government for the purposes of Cites (International Convention on Trade in Endangered Species of Flora and Fauna). In the same year, the influential NATO Conference on the Conservation of Threatened Plants was held at Kew.

In the Gardens the quality of horticultural training was improved, and the School of Horticulture added more science and management to the Diploma curriculum. Glasshouses were renewed and landscaped, and capillary bonding and mist units were installed in 1970. The authenticity of the living collections was reviewed, and a detailed computer-based catalogue prepared. The oil crisis of 1973 led to a complete reappraisal of energy use in the Gardens and new gas and water supplies were laid.

The biochemical work of the Jodrell laboratory has greatly increased in recent years, jointly funded with other bodies. Findings include anti-tumour agents from tropical plants, L-dopa to relieve Parkinson's disease, and castanospermine as an anti-Aids agent.

In 1965 Wakehurst Place in Sussex was acquired on lease from the National Trust. It already had fine collections of trees and shrubs, and it is particularly useful as its soil and rainfall are very different to those at Kew, making it possible to grow plants unsuited to conditions at Kew. These Gardens have been reorganised, converted to scientific and public use, and are becoming increasingly well-known.

Herbarium research was reorganised, and under the Morton Agreement Kew accepted responsibility for floristic and taxonomic work on the tropics, but with global coverage of fungi, grasses and orchids, while the British Museum (Natural History) undertook work on the temperate regions, with global coverage of algae and bryophytes. Kew's collections on these groups were transferred to the Museum for convenience, while the Museum's fungi collections were sent to Kew. A Palynology Unit was set up and electron microscopy utilised to elucidate hitherto intractable problems.

Since 1984, under the provisions of the National Heritage Act 1983, the Royal Botanic Gardens, Kew, have been administered by an independent Board of Trustees, and funded by direct grant from MAFF. Development of facilities to allow achievement of Kew's objectives continues. In 1984 a computer unit was established on-site; in 1987 the Princess of Wales Conservatory was officially opened. This is the world's largest conservatory with 10 different habitats ranging from temperate desert to tropical rain forest; its heating, ventilation and humidity are computer-controlled. The Palm House is being restored and the new Sir Joseph Banks Centre for Economic Botany being built. A Paper Preservation Unit has been established in the Library.

Sadly, the hurricane of 16 October 1987 destroyed about 1,000 trees, including many rare or unique specimens, but even this disaster has been turned to good and the opportunity taken to do extensive root studies and to renovate the collection.

Future plans aim to enhance Kew's excellence and usefulness, and to bring to bear all Kew's resources on important questions. This necessitates the attraction of additional funding by marketing and by use of other charitable sources. Visitors' needs are being reviewed and a wider range of publications prepared for various media; new technology is being applied to create vital databases.

Ultimately mankind is dependent upon plants for a safe environment and adequate economy; the expertise and resources of the Royal Botanic Gardens are an unrivalled and critical resource for improving the quality of life both at home and in other countries.

# 8 FOOD

In the middle of the 19th century adulteration of food was commonplace. Lead was a routine contaminant, bread was adulterated because millstone grit was not removed from the flour, and there were cases involving the mixture of sand and sawdust into the dough. Beer and milk were frequently watered down and other leaves added to tea. There was widespread use of copper, lead, mercury and arsenic pigments as colouring matters in sweets, potted meat and fish and preserved fruit and vegetables. As a result of such revelations, a Committee was appointed to investigate food adulteration and subsequently the Adulteration of Food & Drink Act 1860 was passed – the first general pure food law to be published in any English-speaking country. It made it an offence to sell food containing injurious ingredients or material, and set up local enforcement authorities.

But this Act and an amended Act in 1872 were regarded as failures mainly because of difficulties over sampling arrangements and the lack of qualified men to work as official analysts. The Food & Drugs Act passed in 1875 had more of an impact on food quality, purity and the control of adulteration. This laid down for the first time that 'no person shall sell to the prejudice of the purchaser any article of food or anything which is not of the nature, substance or quality demanded by such purchaser'. The same year the Society of Public Analysts was formed and the foundations thus laid for the supply of analysts with the necessary knowledge and skill to enable food laws to be enforced.

Today the basic legislation is found in Section 1 of the Food Act 1984, which makes it an offence to add any substance to food, or take away any constituent, or subject food to any process or treatment which would make it

*81. Fulsome claims were made in food advertisements at the turn of the century*

injurious to health. The European Community has had a major impact on UK food law; it is moving towards harmonisation of member states' food laws, and many UK regulations have been made under the Food Acts which put EC directives into UK law. Food quality legislation is now enforced by Trading Standards Departments of local authorities, and food hygiene or safety measures by Environmental Health Officers. Port health authorities keep a watch on imported foods.

CUSTARD WITHOUT EGGS!!

BIRD'S CUSTARD POWDER
A Daily Luxury
Supplies the Choicest Dishes

*82. An early convenience food*

Towards the end of the 19th century the nation was largely dependent on staple food such as cereals and potatoes, but consumption of refined sugar, meats and fats rose in the 20th century. Before World War One the UK imported most of its major food commodities, and even in the late 1930s over half our food supplies came from abroad. Writing before World War Two, Sir John Boyd Orr (later Lord Boyd Orr) declared, on the basis of a number of sample family budgets, that the adequacy of diet was related to income. Despite public health measures such as school meals, the school milk scheme and the free issue of milk and vitamins at child clinics, the diet of the two lowest income groups was, he said, grossly inadequate, and although the consumption of cheap foods like bread and sugar was fairly uniform across all classes, consumption of 'protective' foods (milk, other dairy products, vegetables, fruit and eggs) corresponded with family income and was automatically rationed by price. He concluded that the Government should initiate a food policy deliberately contrived to improve the nutrition of the whole population.

When rationing of butter, bacon and sugar was imminent, the Minister of Health and Professor Jack Drummond (Scientific Adviser to the Ministry of Food) separately propounded the view that the war presented a unique opportunity for improving the nation's diet. Research carried out between the wars had improved knowledge of nutritional requirements and practical steps were taken. Vitamins A and D were added to margarine and the National Milk Scheme was aimed at raising the intake of animal protein, calcium and riboflavin in 'vulnerable' groups. People were encouraged to grow carrots and green vegetables.

The higher extraction rate of flour for bread added Vitamin B to the diet, although the 'National Loaf' on sale during the war was popularly held to be responsible for 'the unusual amount of skin rashes, boils . . . and the vast range of disorders at present experienced . . .' The Government's achievement was acknowledged by the award of the Lasker Trophy, presented jointly to the Ministries of Food and Health after the war by the

American Public Health Association in recognition of the way both Ministries were successful in maintaining and improving public health in Great Britain.

The Ministry of Food's Supply Board ran several committees which oversaw the whole pattern of food supply and distribution, and the researchers of the *National Food Survey* evaluated the family food purchases of the 'working class'. Food subsidies kept prices down, and food control helped to raise the standard of living of the poorer section of the community to the level of others. Through the *National Food Survey* a continuing watch is still kept on domestic consumption and dietary trends. Recent evidence shows that people are eating a more nutritious diet containing more green vegetables, fresh fruit and wholemeal bread and are reducing their total calorie intake. The *Survey* is now supplemented by dietary surveys of particular groups such as teenagers, pregnant women and vegetarians.

Today there is a wide choice of both fresh and processed foods, and improvements in storage techniques and production methods have been made. Retail outlets have moved far beyond the corner shop, consumption of the more expensive convenience foods has risen, and novel foods are being developed. Coupled with abundance of choice is a growing public awareness of the dangers of over-eating and a reversion to healthier eating habits.

Exaggerated health claims were made on food labels and in advertisements around the turn of the century that would not be countenanced today. Nevertheless, the UK has been concerned with food labelling at least since the 1890s: the composition, labelling, advertising and description of food generally came within the remit of the Food Standards, Hygiene and Slaughterhouse Policy division in the 1950s when the Ministry of Agriculture and Fisheries and the Ministry of Food were amalgamated. These duties are now laid down by statute in the consolidating Food Act 1984, and in EC rules. New regulations on labelling came into force in 1983 as part of the EC's consumer protection programme; these state that shoppers must be given certain information, including details of quantity, ingredients, datemark and storage conditions, and these must be displayed on the label.

A report produced by a panel of the Committee on Medical Aspects of Food Policy (COMA) on diet and cardiovascular disease, published in 1984, recommended

83. *Wartime food charts from the Ministry of Food*

84. *World War Two poster*

85. *National Milk Scheme provided free milk for the poorest children and expectant mothers*

fat content and nutrition labelling, and in so doing introduced a new concept – that of telling people what effect a particular food will have on their bodies, rather than what it contains. MAFF has proposed a statutory scheme requiring that food should be labelled with its fat content, a requirement which goes beyond that set out in the harmonised EC labelling rules. The aim is to help consumers to select a healthy diet with a wide range of nutrients. However, discussion still continues in the Community on nutritional guidelines.

In the international field the UK has actively participated in agreements on worldwide standards for foods. It is a member of the Codex Alimentarius Commission (the main international food standards organisation, established to implement the joint FAO/WHO Food Standards Programme).

The Codex is a collection of international food standards that aim to protect consumers' health and ensure fair practices in the food trade; it also includes advisory provisions such as codes of practice, guidelines and other recommended measures. Standards have been formulated for all the principal foods for distribution to the consumer, as have provisions concerning food hygiene, additives, pesticide residues, contaminants, labelling, and methods of analysis and sampling.

Before World War Two the main legislative controls over food composition were the Food & Drugs Acts of 1928 and 1938 – in the latter the prevention of adulteration and allied offences were amalgamated with the public health aspects. But with the coming of war a much higher degree of control was required to cope with the consequences of food rationing, shortages of raw materials and the possible introduction of substitute foods. Powers over additions to foods were taken over and extended by Defence regulations. An inter-departmental Committee was set up in 1942 to advise the Ministry of Food on appropriate standards for various foods, but was replaced five years later by the Food Standards Committee. (The minutes of that Committee's first meeting list, among topics discussed, tomato ketchup and curry powder – a modest, if indigestible start.) The Committee continued its work after the merger with MAF and issued numerous reports.

Independent advice about the composition of foods and the acceptability of various additives is now given to the Minister by the Food Advisory Committee (formed in 1983 from the Food Standards Committee and the Food Additives and Contaminants Committee). Additives must be evaluated for safety before they are permitted in food, whereas in earlier times no one would have had the necessary technical and scientific expertise to do this. Some additives, such as preservatives, are necessary to stop microbes from spoiling food, thus preventing wastage and the danger of food poisoning. Others, like emulsifiers and stabilisers, are used in many modern convenience foods. All additives have to go through a long process of approval before they may be used in food. The Food Advisory Committee also advises Ministers on food labelling and advertising questions.

The 1955 Food & Drugs Act sought to ensure that consumers could buy safe, wholesome food and made it an offence to sell for human consumption any food to which substances had been added or removed, or which had been processed to render it injurious to health. The Act also covered provision and regulation of markets, slaughterhouses, knackers' yards and cold stores. The drug provisions of the Act were superseded in 1974 by the Medicines Act 1968, and the Act itself was repealed by the Food Act of 1984.

Apart from its legislative programme, the Ministry has a substantial surveillance role. The Steering Group on Food Surveillance is chaired by MAFF's Chief Scientist, and under the surveillance programme, problems of contamination can be identified and rectified. The present programme includes pesticides, veterinary drug residues, food additives and packaging.

# 9 STATISTICS AND JOURNALS

## STATISTICS

'MY STATISTICAL DEPARTMENT
IS TO BE IMMEDIATELY USEFUL
TO THE AGRICULTURALIST.'
MR CHAPLIN IS REPORTED TO
HAVE OBSERVED IN A HAPPY
COMPARISON FOR THE BENEFIT
OF A SUBORDINATE.

*Mark Lane Express*
14 October 1889

As long ago as the Domesday Survey, a census of land and livestock was taken, and agricultural statistics were collected well before Mr Chaplin's Statistical department began its work. Sir John Sinclair was working on his *Statistical Account of Scotland* in 1791, two years before founding the first Board of Agriculture, and in his inaugural address to the Board had stressed the importance of instituting an agricultural survey of every county. However, the Board's instructions to surveyors did not ask for detailed statistical information and indeed, according to the Secretary, Arthur Young, 'it was morally impossible to find any merit attaching to by far the greater part of them ... and a more wretched mass of erroneous and insufficient information could scarcely have been produced'.

In 1845 the Government attempted to collect agricultural statistics in certain areas of England, Scotland and Ireland. Milner Gibson, then Vice-President of the Board of Trade, introduced a Bill to make provision for collecting such figures in 1847, but it failed at the first reading and was dismissed as 'wild and useless'. A Select Committee investigating the best way of obtaining accurate agricultural information prefaced its findings in 1855 with the remark that 'the importance of obtaining accurate returns ... is now so generally admitted that it appears to the Committee scarcely necessary to dwell upon it'.

National statistics were first collected on a voluntary basis in 1866 by the Inland Revenue's Excise Officers on behalf of the Board of Trade; £10,000 had been voted by Parliament for this task. The work was begun at a time of crisis in the industry when rinderpest was devastating the country and it was estimated that well over 400,000 cattle out of a total of 6 million had died. Accurate returns of horned cattle and sheep were needed to assess the extent

86. *Livestock returns were first published in May 1866, followed by crops and grass statistics in December 1866*

of the damage. First published were the livestock returns in May 1866, followed by crops and grass statistics in December; together these returns constituted the first annual agricultural census. Not all farmers were co-operative – the Inland Revenue's annual report for 1868 comments: 'the duty of collecting these statistics is very harassing to the officers and exposes them to much insult and annoyance'. Not for 10 years did the response rate reach a satisfactory level.

In 1883 responsibility for the returns was transferred to the new Agricultural Department of the Privy Council, although the Board of Trade and the Inland Revenue continued to do the work, and a year later a system of estimating the yields and production of the most important crops was introduced. The newly established Board of Agriculture took over publication of the statistics in 1889, but the Inland Revenue continued their collection until 1919, when the Ministry of Agriculture began to use its own reporters.

The annual reports grew longer over the years, and by 1906 the census covered acreage and livestock returns, crop production, supply and prices of produce, and comparative colonial and foreign statistics. Until 1917 it was conducted on a voluntary basis, but war and the Corn Production Act 1917 necessitated a compulsory return, and this was continued by the 1925 Agricultural Returns Act.

Over the years the replies received from farmers and small holders have been of varying usefulness. Sir Francis Floud (Permanent Secretary 1920–27) recalls in his history of the Ministry some of the more striking answers to census questions; in one case the answer was: 'the cattle are cross-bred, some take after the bull, some after the cow, and the bull sometimes takes after the cowman'. Inquiries as to the motive power used on farms elicited replies of: 'a wheelbarrow', 'a cart', and 'swearing'. One farmer objected: 'these questions are getting too personal and too much Lloyd George'.

The agricultural census, taken every June, remains the most important source of information on agriculture, covering acreage of principal crops, numbers of livestock and of the labour force. Smaller censuses are also carried out in December, March and September, and minor inquiries made from time to time. Forms are received by post and when completed are returned to the Agricultural Departments; summarised results are published each year in *Agricultural Statistics*. Census results are used for estimates of production and studies on the structure of the industry and an estimate of farm income and output is also produced for the Annual Review.

The number of items on the return has varied over the years, from 22 in 1866 to 146 a century later – new items and other changes are referred to the Agricultural Statistics Consultative Committee chaired by MAFF, which represents the interests of landowners, farmers and workers. Crop yield reports are recorded by local officers

*87. Sir Francis Floud, Permanent Secretary to the Ministry of Agriculture and Fisheries, 1920–27*

around the country, and market reports on fat, store and breeding stock are collected at livestock auction markets; reports on eggs, and poultry and information on fruit, vegetables and flowers are sent in from wholesale markets. The Home-Grown Cereals Authority and the Meat & Livestock Commission now act as MAFF's agents in collecting statistical information.

The Annual Review of Agriculture is published as a command paper, setting out data considered during the annual review of economic conditions and prospects of the UK agricultural industry. It covers the main aspects of the industry and the contribution it makes to the national economy. The Government makes use of this information when assessing proposals from the European Commission for agricultural support in the year ahead, and when taking decisions on national support arrangements.

Other statistical series include *Farm incomes in the UK*, which publishes the results of the Farm Management Survey (started in 1936 with the aim of filling 'a gap in our economic knowledge of agriculture'); 2,700 farms in England and Wales are surveyed, plus farms in Scotland and Northern Ireland. Twelve universities and colleges and the Northern Ireland Department of Agriculture conduct the survey and its results are valued for their impartial and broad coverage of the farming industry. A variety of Press Notices give agricultural statistical data, and Wages & Employment inquiries into earnings and hours worked are conducted continuously by MAFF and the Department of Agriculture for Scotland; this information is published in the Department of Employment *Gazette* and *Bulletin*.

## FISHERIES STATISTICS

Responsibility for fisheries passed in part to the Board of Agriculture in 1903. It was the business of the department to 'acquire knowledge of fisheries, fishermen, fishing and fish, [and] to place this information at the disposal of executive departments as occasion required'. The Statistical branch at that time consisted of staff in London and Lowestoft, and of collectors of statistics in all the main fishing ports. These supplied the bulk of material from which the monthly returns of sea fisheries and annual statistical tables were compiled. Information was, and is, available on the quantities and varieties of fish landed, market prices, the amount of fishing in various grounds, and fish stocks.

There is a MAFF presence at each port where there are significant landings of fish, and all vessels over 10 metres must keep a log book. MAFF also keeps a record of each registered fishing vessel.

## FOOD STATISTICS

During World War One, statistical work on supplies of food and foreign agriculture greatly increased. In August 1914, information was obtained on home-grown supplies, returns of stock purchased, and prices of the principal agricultural commodities. A Special Inquiries Branch was set up and transferred to the Ministry of Food upon its creation in 1917, with the duty of collecting all available information as to food resources and the effect of war on farming generally.

During World War Two, the Ministry of Food created a Food Supply Board, with committees covering imports, home production, utilisation and so on. Its Freights Committee obtained weekly statements giving three-month forecasts for anticipated arrivals of each commodity; the Imports Committee received regular statements of actual arrivals, and the Home Agricultural Supplies Committee collected periodical statements showing how home production appeared likely to match up with targets. The Utilisation Committee received details of supplies going into rationing, manufacturing, catering, industrial and service sectors.

But probably the best known series of food statistics was the National Food Survey Committee's annual report on household food consumption and expenditure which includes data obtained from sample households in Great Britain. The series began in July 1940, to provide an independent check on the food consumption and expenditure of the population during the war, so as to assess the effectiveness of the Government's wartime food policy. It was assumed that this would be most clearly reflected in urban working-class households, and would show how they were managing under rationing and food control. It was intended to act as an early warning system of any inadequacies that might result from shortages and changes in diet.

Small samples of middle-class households were added in the mid- and late-1940s, and the survey was again extended in 1950 to cover other social and income groups. The 1950 report included data on expenditure as well as consumption, energy value and nutrient content of foods and material on the household diet of different social classes and differing family composition, drawing comparisons with pre-war survey information.

Material from the *National Food Survey* remains an invaluable source for examining the nutritional and economic status of the more vulnerable groups such as large families on low incomes who have not fully shared in the general rise in the standard of diet. Other statistical series include MAFF's *Food Facts*, which release figures for total food supplies moving into consumption, and the results of the *National Food Survey*, as well as other statistical information.

# JOURNALS

The Board of Agriculture, since its inception in 1889, had been in the habit of issuing 'from time to time, as the necessity arose', leaflets dealing with pests and insects harmful to agriculture. In 1890, Major Craigie of the Animals division, submitted a memo on the practicability of issuing a quarterly journal. His proposal proved unsuccessful, but in July 1893 formal application was made to the Treasury for permission to produce such a publication, on the lines of the *Board of Trade Journal*. The Treasury were unenthusiastic and more correspondence passed until in June 1894 permission was given to publish experimentally for a limited period with financial support up to March 1895.

So, five years after its founding, the Board began to issue the quarterly *Journal of the Board of Agriculture* 'with the double object of providing a suitable channel for giving publicity to such information [of interest to agriculturalists] and securing a medium for systematically recording certain statistical and other intelligence . . .' Material was published on the state of agriculture in the colonies and elsewhere, drawn from reports from foreign governments, diplomatic and consular despatches, research results, and news of any noteworthy inventions in methods of marketing and distributing agricultural produce. Statistics on imports, exports and prices would also be issued.

The first number could hardly have appeared at a more difficult time for farmers; the state of agriculture was extremely depressed, and the price of wheat was at its lowest level since corn returns began in 1771. Somewhat tactlessly, the first issue included an article on the cost of growing wheat in the United States, one on crop prospects abroad, and another on poultry rearing in Russia. However, the President approved, minuting the file on 3rd

*88. First issue of the* Journal of the Board of Agriculture

**BULLETIN**

OF THE MINISTRY OF AGRICULTURE, FISHERIES AND FOOD

No. 1                                        April 1957

*A Message*

*from*

*The Minister*

I am very glad that the Department is going to publish a staff Bulletin. We are a big organization, and our members are scattered over the whole country. But we are all contributing to the same job—of seeing that the country is well fed and the countryside in good heart.

I always think, if one is a member of a big organization, it is interesting to know what one's colleagues are up to and how one's own bit fits into the collective effort. So I think a Bulletin of this kind should prove interesting and useful to us all.

I welcome too the opportunity this Bulletin gives me of saying to you all how grateful I am for the loyal service you have given me whilst I have been in office. It has not been an easy period for any of us, and the fact that we have come through it successfully so far is a great tribute to the teamwork of our Department.

*89. Derick Heathcoat Amory, Minister of Agriculture and Fisheries 1954, and Minister of Food 1954; Minister of Agriculture, Fisheries and Food 1955–1958*

# THE COLORADO BEETLE.

BEETLE

GRUB

EGGS

## A DANGEROUS FOREIGN POTATO PEST.

If you find insects resembling those shown above, please send specimens at once to the Ministry of Agriculture, 10, Whitehall Place, London, S.W.1.

*90. An early Colorado Beetle warning leaflet*

September 1894 as follows: 'The Journal seems very satisfactory. I am glad to see that "petite culture" is referred to, and that any information respecting the home cultivation of eggs, poultry, etc. will be kept in mind in future publications.'*

The first issue was priced at 6d, annual subscription 3/– including postage. The costs of the three experimental issues amounted to £505.3s.4d. with advertisement receipts of £372. No figures are available for sales. The Treasury sanctioned the *Journal*'s continuation in April 1895 and in February 1897 approved a revised scheme whereby it would be published at 1/– a quarter and each number was to consist of no more than 150 pages of literary matter and 25 pages of tables. It was to be circulated via the usual trade channels and railway

bookstalls. The *Journal* became a monthly in 1904, and in 1926 its publication was handed over to HMSO, with the Ministry retaining full editorial control.

During World War One the *Journal* carried articles of particular interest in wartime, such as the monthly notes on feedingstuffs and fertilisers, official information and circulars. It changed its name to *Agriculture* in 1953 and

* MAF 45/2

continued to disseminate information and advice and discuss new developments in farming and food production until its demise in 1972, overtaken by the growth in the number of technical publications currently issued. These included those produced by MAFF's own professional, scientific and technical staff.

The first issue of the Ministry's *Bulletin* came out in April 1957 and grew out of the merger with the Ministry of Food to explain, among other things, what the new amalgamated Ministry would do. This house journal was, said the first editor, by general agreement intended to be formal and official and had to print material that would otherwise be circulated in the Office Notice series. So the first issue contained a reproduction of the Minister's statement on the Annual Review, five pages of parliamentary news and an analysis of the revised fatstock guarantee schemes. There was no editorial comment, no letters, competitions or humour. Gradually articles became lighter and more entertaining; pictures appeared, and in 1964, changes in paper and layout. The *Bulletin* now includes colour material, contributions from all parts of the Ministry, news and photographs.

The Fisheries Laboratory at Lowestoft issued its *Fishery Investigations* series from 1913, covering salmon and freshwater fisheries, sea fisheries and hydrography. Other regular series included *Laboratory leaflets* aimed to 'provide information of immediate practical value to the fishing industry' which could be based on research by the Laboratory or summarise information from all available sources on subjects of current importance. Laboratory technical leaflets, technical reports and fisheries notices were issued, and an annual report on fisheries research is published.

The Ministry also produced other regular publications, many of a technical nature, such as the *NAAS Quarterly Review* (continued as the *ADAS Quarterly Review*) which started in 1948 and was intended to keep agricultural advisers' knowledge up to date with progress and the results of research and experimental work. *Plant Pathology* was a record of current work on plant diseases and pests which was published quarterly for MAF for thirty years from 1952 onwards, and is now produced by the British Society for Plant Pathology. There are numerous other divisional publications and notes, videos and posters available from the Publications branch at Alnwick.

The recent outbreaks of SWINE FEVER in Great Britain were caused mainly by the feeding of unprocessed waste food and demonstrate the dangers of such a practice, particularly the feeding of table or kitchen scraps to pigs.

To help prevent a similar happening in future, the feeding of scraps to livestock and poultry has now been banned.* Only waste food which has been processed by a licensed waste-food operator can be fed to livestock or poultry.

The penalty for breaking this law could be a fine of up to £2000 and offenders could be responsible for causing a serious disease outbreak.

**DO NOT FEED SCRAPS OR ANY UNPROCESSED WASTE FOOD TO ANY OF YOUR FARM LIVESTOCK OR POULTRY**

Although there is no ban on the feeding of scraps which consist of nothing but vegetables or bread, these too could be dangerous if the scraps have been in contact with meat or poultry; so no scraps at all should be fed to livestock or poultry.

*The Diseases of Animals (Waste Food) (Amendment) Order 1987

Prepared for the Ministry of Agriculture, Fisheries and Food by the Central Office of Information 1987
MAFF J0174NJ

*91. MAFF publicity leaflet*

# 10 PEOPLE

## WOMEN IN AGRICULTURE

*BACK TO THE LAND, WE MUST
ALL LEND A HAND,
TO THE FARMS AND THE FIELDS
WE MUST GO.
THERE'S A JOB TO BE DONE.
THOUGH WE CAN'T FIRE A GUN
WE CAN STILL DO OUR BIT WITH
THE HOE.*

From: Land Army song
*Back to the land,* World War Two

The first issue of *The Woman's Agricultural Times*, the official monthly organ of the Agricultural Association of Women, put forward compelling arguments in 1899 for letting women work on the land. Its editor, the Countess of Warwick, wrote about her hostel in Reading where in 1898 12 students lived while attending classes at Reading College on horticulture and the 'lighter branches of agriculture', and carried out practical work in the hostel garden, local nurseries, dairies and poultry farms.

Soon after the outbreak of World War One and the recruitment of male agricultural workers into the forces, it became apparent that women would have to play an active part in agriculture as in other industries. The initial difficulty was for them to obtain enough training and experience to make them useful on the land. (The agricultural education conference report of 1915 had found that the system of education for women that was 'inadequate for normal times, was quite incapable of meeting the demand brought about by the war for a large increase in the facilities for training women to undertake farm work'.) Accordingly some enrolled as short-term students at agricultural colleges where two-to-four week courses were specially run for them, others arranged their practical work on individual farms and still more turned to horticulture. At first, said Miss Macqueen, chief education adviser of the Women's branch of the Food Production Department, employers were much more inclined to look with favour on the woman gardener than on the woman farm labourer.

Lord Selborne, when President of the Board of Agriculture, asked the Board of Trade to co-operate with the War Agricultural Committees already established in every county, to recruit female labour and to set up

*92. Women students at Studley College*

93. World War One poster

94. Recruitment poster for the Women's Land Army

95. '. . . the farmers are depending more and more upon the help of women to increase their crops and look after their cattle . . .' The Landswoman, January 1918

Women's Agricultural Committees, and in 1916 the Women's Organisation was transferred to the Board of Agriculture. Women 'of the educated class' were being enrolled as members of the Women's National Land Service Corps and, shortly after Mr Prothero's appointment as President, he set up the Food Production Department with a Women's branch that took over the organisation of the Women's County Committees. It was 'essential that in future women should be given a voice at headquarters – in the administration of matters which intimately concern the welfare and prosperity of a large number of women throughout the country'.

The Women's Land Army did not come into being until March 1917, when food supplies had dwindled almost to vanishing point. Training of the volunteers recruited by the National Service Department and the Labour Exchanges, was extended to all types of farm work, including afforestation and tractor-driving. The Women's War Agricultural Committees organised and ran the Land Army during 1917, and 1918, and dealt with the training of the girls.

Life in the Women's Land Army consisted mainly of hard work and strict rules, despite the attractive pictures on the recruitment posters and in Government publicity. The organisers were very conscious of their responsibility for their charges: 'The necessity for rigorous control of women for the Land Army is admitted. The supply of girls of sufficiently high character to make it safe to send them out to live alone on the farms or in cottages is running short . . . reports of bad behaviour are becoming more frequent and we are seriously alarmed that at any moment some scandal about the Land Army may break out and the Department be blamed for its inadequate supervision.'*

* MAF 42/8

Miss Talbot, director of the Women's Branch, suggested that hostels be set up for the girls, and that travelling welfare officers should be appointed at £3 a week to investigate problems. Certainly some counties seemed to look on their workers as schoolgirls. The Herts County Land Army handbook's draft rules state:
'1. No member is allowed to enter the bar of a public house.
2. Members must be in their billets for the night by 9.30 p.m.
3. Members are not allowed to smoke while at work, or in any public place when in uniform . . .'

The author attempts to arouse patriotic fervour in the jargon of the time. 'The letters on your badge stand for Land Army Agricultural Section; they also stand for the four gifts of the Land Army: Loyalty, Ability, Ardour, Service.'

But at Headquarters they strongly disapproved of some of the harsh punishments meted out to recalcitrant girls. For example, a newspaper cutting of summer 1918 relates that 'G– S–, a native of Bristol, and belonging to the Women's Army Forage Department was at Gloucester on Friday sent to prison for 14 days' hard labour for being absent from work without leave'.

However, enthusiastic articles about personal experiences working on the land appeared often in contemporary issues of magazines such as *The Landswoman* and *The Lady*. 'If you ask any of the women whether they find the work hard and tiring, they will tell you this encouraging fact; that the regular work in the open air, in sun and rain and wind, brings the needed strength with it . . . after a few days . . . muscles came into line and the work became a real delight.' The sentiments of many farmers are represented in the comments of one southerner: 'I should feel that I had lost a rare thing if I let the girls go, and there's many a farmer I know who will say the same thing when the time comes'.

Women worked in agriculture, horticulture, timber supply and forage, and were given a minimum wage plus their clothing and boots. After the Armistice and the early release of agricultural workers from the Forces, recruiting for the Land Army ceased and the organisation was disbanded. Lord Ernle (formerly Rowland Prothero) wrote then that in all these branches of work 'women have excelled' and 'in driving motor tractors they have done at

*96. Recruitment poster for the Women's Land Army*

least as well as men. Here also light hands tell. As drivers they have shown themselves not only skilful and enduring, but economical'.

In contrast to World War One, when the Women's Land Army was not formed until 1917, proposals were made before World War Two for the setting up of a similar organisation in early 1939, and women not already working on farms full-time were invited to enrol for service. In May 1939, the Minister formally appointed a number of Women's Land Army Voluntary County Committees to start recruiting and training workers. Their task was made easier by the keenness of some girls, recalled Vita Sackville-West in her history of the Land Army; one girl was rung up on 1st September and asked to hold herself in readiness. ' "How long can you give me?" she asked, "twenty minutes?" '

97. *'You may depend upon it that the example you are setting will encourage still more women and girls to find their war work in farming...'*
R Dorman-Smith writing in
The Land Girl, *May 1940*

On the outbreak of war, MAF assumed responsibility for the Women's Land Army and it 'can have had no kinder or more co-operative friend than the Minister of Agriculture, Mr Robert Hudson'. The new organisation was staffed entirely by women, its director being Lady Denman; it had headquarters and county offices, and dealt with recruitment, intensive four-week courses, welfare and accommodation, provision of uniforms and employment. A land girl's duties were various, according to Vita Sackville-West: 'She milks; she does general farm-work . . . in more specialised ways she prunes and sprays fruit-trees, picks and packs the fruit, makes and lays thatch, makes silage, pulls flax, destroys rats . . . works in the forests felling timber . . . it is quite an impressive list.'

Volunteers were employed by individual farmers, and also on gangs directly under the War Ags, the official minimum wage was 48/– and they had seven days leave a year. In 1941 a small itinerant field service was inaugurated to take on seasonal work and in 1942 a Timber Corps was established. Between September 1939 and March 1950, when recruiting ceased, more than 200,000 women had served in the Land Army's ranks. The free uniform consisted of khaki coat, skirt, breeches and stockings, grey pullover, heavy shoes and red and green armlet, although supplies were often short. In 1943 Mr Hudson was asked in Parliament about this and replied: 'We have been fortunate in obtaining some thousands of coats from the ATS, though we might have got more had it not been for the unexpected fact that the conformation of members of the Women's Land Army in material particulars is substantially different from that of the ATS.'

The organisation was kept on to cover the transitional period from war to peace, and recruitment continued. Government advertisements called for help with harvests and fruit and potato picking, and holiday work camps were heavily promoted. The Voluntary Committees were dissolved in 1948 and the whole organisation disbanded in November 1950.

# WORKERS, EMPLOYERS AND THE UNIONS

*HE USED TO TRAMP OFF TO HIS
WORK,
WHILE TOWN FOLK WERE ABED,
WITH NOTHING IN HIS BELLY
BUT A SLICE OR TWO OF BREAD;
HE DINED UPON POTATOES, AND
HE NEVER DREAMT OF MEAT
EXCEPT A LUMP OF BACON FAT
SOMETIMES BY WAY OF TREAT...*

Nineteenth century union ballad

An Agricultural Labourers Union was formed in 1833 at
Tolpuddle in Dorset at a time when wages had been
reduced to 7/– a week – below even their former meagre
level; a year later the six now celebrated leaders were
imprisoned and sent to Botany Bay. Thereafter the union
movement was in the doldrums for many years and did not
really emerge again until 1866 when unions were established in Kent, Bucks, Herefordshire and Hertfordshire.
Joseph Arch, much later MP for North West Norfolk, was
one of those instrumental in getting the movement on its
feet; he undertook agricultural work of all kinds and talked
to labourers around the country about wages and conditions, 'dropping in the good seed of manly discontent'. A
union was soon formed in Warwickshire with Arch as its
leader and 200 members voted to strike for a wage of 16/–
a week for an 11-hour working day.

The National Agricultural Labourers' Union was set up
in May 1872 with a membership that had grown to nearly
50,000 in three months. Members demanded higher
wages, reduction of the working day and education for
young farm workers. Farmers responded with lock-outs
and were supported by clergy and magistrates. They
refused to make any concessions and membership of the
union fell, although in 1884 agricultural labourers received
the vote and with it a little more power. The NALU, beset
by falling rolls, was dissolved in 1896.

A new organisation, the Eastern Counties Agricultural
Labourers and Small Holders Union, was formed in 1906
by George Edwards, a Liberal Party speaker, with
predominantly Liberal officers. Again, it demanded wage
reform, better conditions of employment and rural housing
and land for workers through legislation. In 1909 it
changed its name to the National Agricultural Labourers

*98. Joseph Arch, trade unionist and MP for N W Norfolk*

and Rural Workers Union, reiterating claims for higher wages and reduced working hours, and in 1920 became the National Union of Agricultural Workers. In 1968 it was transformed into the National Union of Agricultural and Allied Workers and became a separate trade group within the Transport and General Workers' Union in 1982.

Ministers were aware of the workers' hardships well before World War One. When Walter Runciman was President of the Board (1911–1914) he had commented on the lack of offers for small holdings. 'There were very few labourers among the applicants', he noted, 'because the low wages paid to agricultural workers did not enable them to lay by even the small amount of capital required . . .' The National Farmers Union supported his wish for a conference to be held on the problems of agriculture, and a Land Enquiry Committee set up by Lloyd George in 1912 found that 'there is an urgent need in every county for labourers' cottages . . . the condition of many of the existing cottages is most unsatisfactory'.

The only other agricultural labourers' union of significance was the Workers' Union. In 1889 it began recruiting farmworkers and managed to raise wages by one to three shillings a week; in its heyday in 1919 it had over 100,000 members. Between them the two unions had thousands of members, but despite that, *The Times* could comment disparagingly: 'as a class . . . the agricultural labourers of this country are an unorganised body, incapable of concerted action in a national strike movement, for comparatively few of them are yet enrolled on the books of a trade union'.

The employers were also organising themselves and the National Farmers' Union was founded in December 1908 having its origins in the Lincolnshire Farmers' Union. It was, said the Secretary: 'the first genuine effort on the part of farmers themselves to combine for their own protection and benefit . . . Surely a Government or a Board of Agriculture would give greater attention to the voice of the farmers on farming questions than to that of a mixed body.' The NFU was formed because it was thought that the farming interest had been neglected by both political parties. A 1907 pamphlet issued by the pioneer Lincolnshire Farmers' Union declared: 'It must be remembered that, however bitterly the two great parties of State were opposed on many questions, as regards agriculture they

99. *A page from the minute book of the Lincolnshire Farmers' Union, forerunner of the NFU*

were equally indifferent; the one side counting on the unreasoning support, and the other side on the bitter opposition of the farmers.'

The NFU grew from 10,000 members in 1908 to over

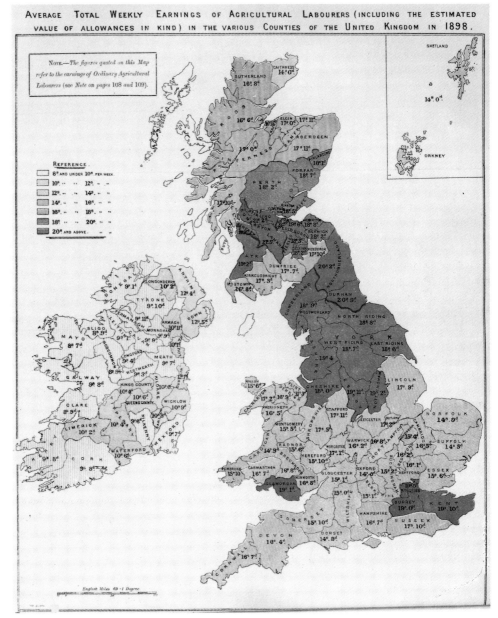

100. Average weekly earnings of
agricultural workers at the end of
the 19th century

100,000 by 1921. In World War One it was called on to help in the effort to increase food production, and in the second it played an active part in running the County War Agricultural Committees. It also had a consultative and advisory role, taking part, after the war, with the Agricultural Departments, in reviewing annually the general financial position of UK agriculture and the fixing of prices. It is now the major national organisation representing farmers and growers, and an influential pressure group at local, national and international level.

WAGES AND CONDITIONS
Before 1917, the Board of Agriculture had no specific duties with regard to labour and wages. The Corn Production Act of that year gave it responsibility for establishing machinery to fix a minimum agricultural wage of 25/– a week and provided for an Agricultural Wages Board to administer this and hear complaints, but the Wages Board had a short life, being abolished by the passing of the Corn Production Acts (Repeal) Act 1921, which was widely viewed as a betrayal of the farmers and their immense war effort – and of their workers. In a penitential 'white sheet' Lord Clinton, Parliamentary Secretary, brought the Bill before the House of Lords, declaring: 'I have admitted at the very beginning that this Bill is a breach of faith which I regret to bring forward . . .'

The Act repealed the guaranteed price provisions of 1917: 'Agriculture will be entirely decontrolled and guaranteed prices, control of cultivation and the Wages Board will all disappear after the coming harvest', declared the Minister, Sir Arthur Griffith Boscawen, on the second reading. The Wages Board was replaced with voluntary conciliation and MAF duties became purely advisory. The statutory minimum wage system was reintroduced in the Labour Government's Agricultural Wages (Regulation) Act 1924, with administration being retained by the Ministry, and a Central Wages Board and Agricultural Wages Committees concerned with determination of minimum rates and framing the orders. Committees were made up of representatives of employers appointed by the NFU, of workers chosen by the National Union of Agricultural Workers and the Workers Union, and of independent members familiar with the industry selected by the Minister.

Before World War Two, the statutory minimum wage averaged 34/6d, although this varied from county to county. By 1939 hours were regulated and workers enjoyed a weekly half-holiday, limited annual leave and unemployment insurance. With war, agriculture once more became vitally important and wages rose rapidly; by March 1945 they were 70/– a week. The Agricultural Wages Board for England and Wales has in recent years introduced a wages structure into the industry to allow higher minimum rates of pay for craftsmen and supervisors, and has also instituted a sick pay system for agricultural workers. Throughout its existence it has remained independent of Ministers.

Legislation on the health, welfare and safety of agricultural workers is more recent than that governing rates of pay. The Agriculture (Poisonous Substances) Act 1952 was introduced because of the many accidents arising from the use of new sprays for killing weeds, and empowered the Minister to make regulations on the wearing of protective clothing by workers using dangerous chemicals. Farmers were responsible for ensuring that the necessary equipment was provided. The Agriculture (Safety, Health & Welfare Provisions) Act 1956 provided for regulations safeguarding agricultural workers against injury and risk to health, and for the protection of children. Over the years the Ministry has been closely involved with the health and safety of those working in the industry.

The Health & Safety at Work etc., Act 1974 places general obligations of care and protection on employers, employees, the self-employed, and manufacturers and suppliers of plant and material. This protection extends to all, including the general public, who may be affected by farm activities. The Ministry tries to build up safety consciousness in the industry by using education, advice and publicity in leaflets, films, broadcasts and the press. The MAFF Advisory Committee on Pesticides reviews risks from the use of pesticides, veterinary chemicals and any potentially toxic chemicals referred to it by Ministers.

# 11 EDUCATION AND RESEARCH ESTABLISHMENTS

The 18th century had been notable for the work of such men as Robert Bakewell the experimental agriculturalist, 'Turnip Townshend' and the Earl of Leicester, Thomas Coke, who received a gold medal from the first Board of Agriculture for his extensive irrigation system at Lexham in 1806. Last, but not least, came Arthur Young, first secretary of the first Board of Agriculture: 'to him more than to any other individual were due the dissemination of new ideas on farming, the diffusion of the latest results of observation and experiment'.

The Board of Agriculture Act 1889 authorised the Board to inspect and provide (very limited) financial assistance to the three schools then teaching agriculture. To begin with, the Parliamentary grant of £5,000 was allocated in the form of small grants to existing institutions, and the first college to receive financial aid was the University College of North Wales at Bangor.

The opportunity to develop agricultural instruction on a more generous scale came about in 1890 with the 'whisky money'. In that year additional duties were imposed on beer and spirits, the proceeds being intended partly for grants to the local authorities for police purposes, and partly for the revocation with compensation of liquor licences. The latter aroused such fury that the proposals had to be withdrawn and the whisky money, amounting to £750,000 a year, was paid into the local taxation account for distribution to county councils who were authorised to use it for technical, including agricultural, instruction.

Some did not accede to this, but many councils used the money to establish lectures, travelling schools, instruction, dairy schools and grants to new or existing colleges. The Board of Agriculture allocated small funds primarily to central institutions and planned to establish centres, each

*101. Robert Bakewell, experimental agriculturalist: 'Every branch of agricultural art was more or less indebted to him, his fortunate genius and his original mind.'*

101

associated with a university if possible, evenly over the country. Colleges were set up at Leeds, Newcastle, Aberystwyth, Cambridge, Nottingham, Reading and Wye by 1896.

The Reay Committee reported in 1908 on existing provision for science and technical instruction and concluded that although there were by then enough institutions, better staff and equipment were required, while facilities for lower level teaching were unsystematic and inadequate. It recommended that farm institutes should be set up to provide winter courses for young agricultural workers, and that resident agricultural advisers should be appointed in each county-size area, to give information and instruction to farmers.

In 1910 the newly appointed Development Commissioners were made responsible for distribution of the then huge sum of £2.9 million for the development of agriculture, forestry, harbours and fisheries. £325,000 was set aside for the development of farm institutes, enabling the Board of Agriculture to make grants to county councils of 75% of the capital cost of providing an institute and up to 50% of the annual maintenance costs. Responsibility for farm institutes and other agricultural education financed from the Development Fund was passed to the Board of Agriculture in 1912.

During the war some grants were suspended, but others continued, as far as limitations of staff and shortage of male students allowed. Many colleges were used to train women in farm work and give courses for allotment holders on the techniques of vegetable growing.

Between 1919–21, six new farm institutes were established and a further five in the next six years. Gradually agricultural teaching was built up through the colleges and agricultural departments of universities, and also by the county councils' agency organisers and instructors.

The Agricultural Improvement Council for England and Wales was founded in 1941 to advise the Minister on the investigation of technical problems in agriculture and the dissemination of research results, and to devise methods of applying these to farming practice.

Since 1947, financial assistance for agricultural departments in universities has been included in UGC grants while farm institutes and other agricultural education activities of local authorities have been within the remit of the Department of Education & Science since 1959. The

*102. Safety leaflet*

Ministry retained responsibility for the independent Royal Agricultural College of Cirencester and the directly grant-aided colleges: Harper Adams, Seale Hayne, Shuttleworth and Studley (now closed) until 1964.

The system built up before World War Two provided for state aid for research, for advisory work with farmers, and for agricultural education. As the work of the research institutes developed, the need for a scientific co-ordinating authority led, in 1931, to the establishment by Royal

103. *Studley College: women students in the vineyard*

Charter of the Agricultural Research Council to advise the agriculture departments. With expansion of research after the war, it became clear that a single body in charge of all government-aided research was required and in 1956 the Council was given statutory authority. It is now known as the Agricultural and Food Research Council, and is funded through the science budget via DES, and income from work commissioned by MAFF. Four members of MAFF are Council members – the Deputy Secretary (Land and Resources), the Chief Scientific Adviser, and the two Chief Scientists. The Chief Veterinary Officer is an assessor to the Council.

The Ministry's interest in educational matters also extends to vocational training. The National Farmers' Union first suggested that there should be an Agricultural Training Board, and this body was established in 1966 to train those involved in commercial agriculture and horticulture in Great Britain. With the Industrial Training Boards it was the responsibility of the Department of Employment until it became linked with MAFF and the other agricultural Departments in 1975. To this day the majority of its income is provided by MAFF grant-in-aid.

In 1968, after the foot-and-mouth epidemic, the Board offered practical training courses to help farmers considering diversification and also assumed responsibility for administering apprenticeship schemes. In recent years the Board's remit has been widened by legislation to permit it to operate overseas (as the British Agricultural Training Board) and to train farmers in Great Britain to enable them to widen their businesses.

# MINISTRY RESEARCH ESTABLISHMENTS

## DIRECTORATE OF FISHERIES RESEARCH

The origin of fisheries research dates back to the second half of the 19th century. The Marine Biological Association was formed in 1884, and opened fisheries laboratories in Plymouth and Grimsby to study the state of fishing grounds in the Channel and the North Sea. The problem of maintaining fish stocks was discussed at several international meetings and the International Council for the Exploration of the Sea (ICES) was set up in 1902 as a forum for the exchange of information and ideas on the sea and its living resources, and for the promotion and co-ordination of research.

The first English fisheries research vessel was *ST Huxley*, acquired by the Marine Biological Association and used out of Lowestoft for international investigations from 1901 onwards. In 1902 the Association was asked to undertake an investigation of the state of the plaice fishery at the instigation of ICES, and a sub-station was opened at Lowestoft for the purpose. Later, responsibility for the work programme was taken over by the Board of Agriculture in 1908 and transferred to its London offices in Parliament Street. The staff were absorbed into the civil service and moved to London, although Lloyd George had written a personal letter to the then President, Lord Carrington, asking him to ensure that they would be retained to carry out the North Sea work.

In December 1913, the Development Commission was asked to approve a research scheme which included the purchase of three research vessels, new laboratory accommodation, extra staff and motorboats for the culture of lobsters and oysters. With funds from the Commission and the Treasury, the Board carried out research and produced reports from 1910–14 on plaice, North Sea cod and

*104. Director and staff at Lowestoft Laboratory, 1907.* Back row: *Potter, Arrowsmith, Walton, Ansell;* middle row: *James, Nefford, Rosa Lee, Todd, Dykes;* front row: *Wallace, Garstang, Borley, Atkinson*

haddock, and herring. Three series of publications were started: *Fisheries notices* (1911), *Fishery Investigations* Series 1: *Salmon and freshwater fisheries* (1913), and Series II: *Sea fisheries* (1914) but nearly all this work stopped in August 1914. The Development Commission had to cut financial aid to a minimum, but continued to pay the annual research grants.

105. *Cartoon of the Fisheries Laboratory at Lowestoft, by A Hardy, 1921*

In 1915–16, £6,000 was given to the Board for research into the destruction of the slipper limpet pest in the Essex estuaries. A fisheries experimental station was set up at West Mersea and investigated the cleansing of polluted shellfish. In 1915 this work was moved to Conwy, where a practical method of cleansing mussels in sterilised sea water was devised, and in 1916 carried out on a commercial scale.

During World War One, the Fisheries Secretary, Henry Maurice, called together scientists and civil servants to help him start a new research programme; Lowestoft was chosen as the most suitable town and the laboratory opened in converted sea-front premises in 1921, moving to the old Grand Hotel in 1955.

This building is still used today, with the addition of three new wings and a separate block, as the main laboratory of the Directorate. Other laboratories are sited at Burnham-on-Crouch, Conwy and Weymouth. Staff at Lowestoft are concerned with the assessment of all the fish and shellfish stocks fished by the UK industry, carry out work on fish cultivation and on study of the environment in which the fish are found – particularly with regard to the monitoring and control of radioactivity in seawater. At Burnham-on-Crouch research is concentrated upon pro-

tection of the aquatic environment from discharges of non-radioactive pollutants (such as pesticides), and the effects of, for example, offshore oil and marine gravel exploitation. The Conwy laboratory deals with all aspects of coastal fisheries and the Weymouth fish diseases laboratory undertakes research into both marine and freshwater fish.

Fisheries research involves going to sea, and the Directorate has two purpose-built research vessels in operation: *RV Cirolana* (launched in 1970) and *RV Corystes* (launched in 1986). The Directorate carries out research into the aquatic environment, fish stock management and certain aspects of fish cultivation and disease. Staff deal with statutory inspection and environmental research in connection with the control and disposal of radioactive and non-radioactive wastes. They monitor fish quality and assess the levels of fish stocks, study fish behaviour and the physics and chemistry of sea water in relation to fisheries and environmental protection. A history of the Directorate has been written (Lee, 1989) that complements this book.

The present coordinator of fisheries research is the director of the Department of Agriculture & Fisheries for Scotland (DAFS) and the two programmes of research are thus brought together.

*106.* Sir William Hardy, *research trawler used by Torry, and later* known as Rainbow Warrior, *sailing under the Greenpeace flag*

## TORRY RESEARCH STATION, ABERDEEN

Torry Research Station, a laboratory concerned mainly with fish preservation, was founded in 1929 in Aberdeen. Early work was undertaken on the improvement in handling of iced fish and the possibility of trawler-borne freezer installations. A well-known Grimsby trawler owner, Sir John Denton Marsden, was sent a copy of a 1929 report on the handling and storage of white fish at sea and viewed with some dismay the efforts to freeze fish on board '. . . our markets will be open to be exploited by every fish producing country in the world and our people gradually inured to eating frozen fish . . . I hope that it will never come about that the British public will be taught to eat and appreciate frozen fish'.

Work on chilling and freezing techniques and experiments on smoking fish continued until, at the outbreak of war, the laboratory turned to more immediate problems such as the use of fish guts preserved at sea for manufacture of fish meal, and testing vacuum-dried fish and edible fish meal to supplement the dwindling supplies of fresh fish.

After the war a project to freeze whole white fish at sea began, and the method was commercially adopted in 1961. Production and test-marketing of pre-packed chilled fish was carried out, and with the decline in distant-water catches of the late 1960s, staff at Torry began to consider 'non-traditional' species as food. Under MinTech, the laboratory started work on developing all kinds of fishworking machinery and, after a brief spell at the Department of Trade and Industry, Torry moved to MAFF in 1972 and became linked with the fisheries laboratories at Lowestoft and Aberdeen under the aegis of the Controller of Fisheries Research for the UK.

Torry's work also required research facilities at sea and these were often supplied by trawler owners on commercial fishing vessels. More dedicated vessels were sometimes needed and a secondhand drifter, *City of Edinburgh*, was bought in 1930, being superseded by *Keelby* in 1949, in its turn replaced by a custom-built research trawler, *Sir William Hardy*, in 1955. This boat served Torry for over 20 years and was sold, only to reappear under the Greenpeace flag as *Rainbow Warrior*. Torry's last research vessel the *G A Reay* sailed under the MAFF flag until 1984, and currently all sea-going research is done on commercial vessels during commercial fishing trips or under charter.

Today Torry is engaged in research on the handling, processing, preservation and transport of fish and with improving quality at every stage. Torry devised and developed a technique for freezing catches on board, and designed mechanical smoking kilns; staff advise processors on quality control and hygiene, and investigate ways of using fish mince mechanically recovered from the bones and producing from it simulated 'scampi', canned 'salmon' and 'tuna' and composite fish fillets.

In addition, Torry's research programme has always contained a substantial element of background projects designed to shed light on the fundamental physical, chemical and biological properties of fish tissues, particularly so far as their suitability for food is concerned. More recently the laboratory has been given a commercial role and charged with the task of undertaking contract repayment work to offset a substantial proportion of its running costs. Consultancies, analytical and testing services, training and advice are all used to earn receipts.

FOOD SCIENCE LABORATORIES

At present there are three small food laboratories based in London and Norwich. In early 1988 work started on a new building in Norwich, occupying a site next to the Agricultural and Food Research Council's Institute of Food Research; this is due to open in 1989. The Food Science Laboratory represents the tangible part of the Government's efforts to ensure the safety of food as it reaches the consumer, both in shops and in the home; food laws are enforced by local authorities and MAFF's Food Science division carries out surveillance to check whether the law is operating efficiently or whether it needs updating and changing in line with new technology and methods of analysis. (One well-known instance of the division's work is the method of analysis developed by the laboratory and used by enforcement authorities to detect the presence of antifreeze in imported wine.)

Work is also undertaken on pesticide and veterinary residues in food and the presence of heavy metals such as mercury in food. Other research projects orientated towards consumer protection have been on substances leaching out of packaging and into food, notably with the use of clingfilm to cover food in microwave cookers.

All such research is undertaken in the Ministry's own laboratories, and the Minister thus has his own confidential laboratory service. The Food Science Laboratory also acts as the focal point for collaborative studies on trials of proposed new methods of analysis before they are agreed in the EC.

*107. Torry fish tester*

107

## ADAS SLOUGH LABORATORY

The Pest Infestation Laboratory was set up in 1940 by DSIR at the Imperial College Field Station at Slough, to carry out laboratory and field R & D in the prevention and control of insect, mite and fungal pests of stored produce – harvested crops such as cereals, pulses, dried fruits, nuts, oilseeds and cocoa beans. It dealt with imported as well as home-grown commodities. Because the laboratory had only a small staff, inspection and control were undertaken by MAFF.

In 1959, when food research became more centralised, the laboratory was transferred to the Agricultural Research Council, and in 1970 moved to MAFF and became combined with the latter's Infestation Control Laboratory located at Tolworth and Worplesdon. This became part of ADAS in September 1974 and was given responsibility for the work of the Regional Infestation Control Service. Research is carried on at its headquarters in Slough on the biology of insects, mites and fungi associated with stored products, and their control by use of contact insecticides and fumigants. At Tolworth staff investigate the behaviour, ecology and control of rats and other rodents, and at Worplesdon studies are conducted on other harmful mammals and bird pests.

*108. Mink*

*109. Pigeon*

*110. Mould mite*

*111. Housefly*

*Pest research at ADAS Slough Laboratory*

"*A good sign after this wet June – no potato blight, but a drowned Colorado beetle*"

*112. A Colorado Beetle colony was discovered in Britain in 1976*

## ADAS HARPENDEN LABORATORY

The Ministry's Plant Pathology Laboratory was set up in 1918 at the Royal Botanic Gardens Kew, to provide an intelligence and survey service on plant pests and diseases, based on reports from correspondents all over the country. Food shortages and crop losses, and the continuing need for increased food production led to demand for such a service, and at the same time the laboratory was asked to advise the Minister on ways of preventing the introduction of destructive new pests and diseases, and the further spread of dangerous ones already in existence. In 1920 the laboratory moved to a converted private house in Harpenden, and in 1960 transferred to new buildings on its present site at Hatching Green, Harpenden. It came to be recognised as the liaison centre between the research and advisory services and between Government and insecticide and pesticide manufacturers.

The laboratory is now part of the Research & Development Service of ADAS but has strong links with advisory entomologists and plant pathologists. Its scientific and technical responsibilities include research and advice on prevention of entry into England and Wales of plant diseases and pests that attack agricultural and horticultural crops, and containment and eradication of any that do gain entry. The laboratory also has responsibility for the prevention and limitation by statutory means of the spread of established diseases and pests, for health standards for planting material including seeds for the home and export markets, registration of pesticides and evaluation of risk.

# PART III

# 12 MAFF SINCE 1970

## AGRICULTURE

In recent years, the work of MAFF has evolved further in response to changing circumstances which have included notably UK entry to the EC, increases in agricultural production, growing environmental concerns and changes in consumer requirements.

The role of MAFF was substantially altered by the UK accession to the European Community in 1973. Its work changed in character and was much increased, both in quantity and complexity. The then Minister, addressing the Worcester branch of the NFU in 1972, said that the basic aims of the Common Agricultural Policy (CAP) and the Agriculture Act 1947 were much the same – both set out to achieve increased productivity, stable markets and a reasonable standard of living for farmers and farm workers, and assured supplies of food for consumers at reasonable prices. But there the similarities with the traditional support system ended. Under the old system, with certain exceptions such as liquid milk, sugar and potatoes, consumers benefited from prices at or near world levels, and the taxpayer supported farmers through direct subsidies. Even before joining the Community, measures had been introduced to protect UK markets from low-priced imports, but the CAP went much further in managing markets through imposing restrictions on the prices of competing imports.

Under the CAP, support for farmers comes essentially from the price paid by the consumer, and the costs to the taxpayer have arisen mainly from the growth and disposal of surpluses. A system was adopted that applied a common policy of price support and the same marketing arrangements throughout the member states. Producers' incomes are supported partly by levies to maintain minimum prices for imports, partly by measures to help exports, and partly

113. *A familiar Ministry logo*

by internal market support schemes such as intervention buying.

Before accession, national agricultural support policy was implemented by MAFF's commodity divisions. There was a system of annual price bargaining between the Government and the National Farmers' Union, which operated under the provisions of the 1947 Agriculture Act by which deficiency payments were paid in respect of the major commodities. The old system of support still continues where there is no CAP regime. During the run-up to accession, two EC co-ordinating divisions were set up in MAFF and they, together with the commodity divisions, worked out the arrangements for applying Community policy in the UK. Staff had to acquire new language skills and familiarise themselves with products like wine and olive oil which had previously been of little concern to the Ministry. MAFF negotiators encountered many difficulties both before and after accession in adapting to the CAP and have fought a long battle to promote greater economic realism in the system. The development of MAFF's role in Brussels and the need to co-ordinate negotiations going on simultaneously on many related commodity, financial and farm structure issues, has established an *esprit de corps* and a body of negotiating experience and skills in the Department whose quality is recognised in Whitehall generally.

The Intervention Board for Agricultural Produce (IBAP) was set up to deal with the administration of the CAP in the United Kingdom. It is a separate government department with its own accounting officer but under the general direction of the agricultural ministries in England, Scotland, Wales and Northern Ireland. It was initially staffed by a little over 400 officers drawn mainly from MAFF and the members of the Board were appointed to take office on 22 November 1972. It administers and carries out the payments arrangements under the 'guarantee' functions of the CAP, including intervention purchases and sales, production levies, the issue of import/export licenses, payment of export refunds and collection of export levies on Community and third country trade. Schemes for intervention exist for wheat, barley, butter, skimmed milk powder and beef, and the Board has to arrange for stocks bought into intervention to be stored and eventually resold either onto the market or for export. The Home-Grown Cereals Authority and the Meat & Livestock Commission were appointed the executive agents of the Board responsible for ensuring that the market support arrangements for cereals and meat respectively were carried out.

The CAP has stimulated substantially increased production and has provided farmers with higher returns and a better standard of living. But it has also brought problems. High levels of price support have created huge surpluses and intervention buying became an outlet for unlimited production. In 1988 the cost of the CAP was running at £20.6 billion a year and swallowed up 73% of the Community budget. In order to tackle the problems of surpluses and their burgeoning costs, quotas on milk production were introduced in 1984. The following year, the European Commission issued a green paper setting out its views on CAP reform. This revealed a preference for a tough line on price levels rather than an extension of quotas. It discussed ways to promote good management of the environment by farmers, and the possibility of direct income aids for poorer regions. Reduction in milk quotas was introduced in December 1986 and intervention standards were tightened, so making it more difficult for

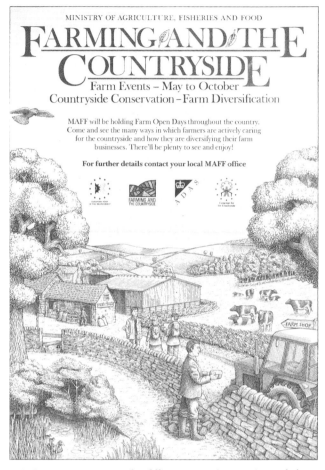

*114. Farmers are encouraged to follow conservation practices and also to diversify into other enterprises benefitting the rural economy*

farmers and traders to offer beef into intervention. In July 1987, support levels for cereals and rapeseed were reduced and subsequently a range of measures was agreed to stabilise the situation and discourage over-production of all the major products.

In the UK today, the agricultural use of land is seen more in the context of the whole environment and the

*115. Farm ponds are encouraged*

organisational structure of the Ministry is being modified and strengthened accordingly. Countryside conservation encompasses many activities that affect the rural environment. The Wildlife & Countryside Act 1981 (and the 1968 Countryside Act before it) laid down that MAFF should give advice to those carrying on agricultural businesses on conservation and enhancement of the 'natural beauty and amenity of the countryside' and on diversification into other enterprises intended to benefit the rural economy. Advice is offered to farmers through ADAS on such matters as the integration of woodland into the management of the farm business, or change of use for redundant farm buildings to be turned into craft centres or farm shops, or used for tourism. A recent MAFF survey revealed that farmers were conservation-conscious and that they involved themselves in the work of Farming and Wildlife Advisory groups. These provide a forum for discussion and problem-solving among farmers, foresters, conservationists and local authorities.

The Agriculture Act 1986 further emphasises the importance of conservation: it requires the Minister to achieve a reasonable balance between agricultural and environmental interests in carrying out his functions in relation to land. It also provides for the establishment of environmentally sensitive areas in which payments are made to farmers for following farming practices which conserve the landscape and habitats. This concept which originated in the UK has been enshrined in Community legislation. So far nineteen areas in the UK have been designated as environmentally sensitive areas and take up by farmers has been very encouraging.

A working party was set up in 1986 by several Government departments, including MAFF, to advise Ministers on the possible alternative uses of land and new jobs in the countryside. The project was code-named ALURE (Alternative Land Use and the Rural Economy) and led to the publication in the spring of 1987 of *Farming and the rural enterprise*. This included proposals for a new woodland scheme to encourage tree-planting as a farm enterprise, for some expansion of the traditional forestry programme and for extra funds for the environmentally sensitive areas. Farmers are being encouraged to diversify into activities making full use of all their assets in land, buildings and people.

New Agriculture Improvement Schemes had been introduced in 1985, the major scheme extending eligibility to small farmers for investments to improve the environment and prevent pollution. Grants are now offered for the setting up of ancillary businesses on farms such as the conversion of buildings to make farmhouse butter and cheese, towards the capital costs of providing tourist accommodation on farms, setting up recreational activities, and for feasibility studies.

During the 1970s, the Ministry also much increased its activities to protect the land and marine environment against pollution. Statutory backing for many of these activities was provided in the Food and Environment Protection Act 1985, which provided powers for emergency actions against contamination of food supplies, for licensing of sea dumping and incineration of waste products at sea and for the control of pesticides.

The Less Favoured Areas cover 53% of agricultural land in the UK and 65,000 farmers receive Hill Livestock Compensatory Allowances while grants of 25% of the cost may be made to hill farmers for tourism and recreation enterprises. Capital grants, assistance for flood defence and arterial drainage, advisory services, research and development, and vocational training through the Agricultural Training Board and agricultural colleges, are also provided.

As the workforce in agriculture has declined, MAFF has developed a wider interest in job opportunities in rural areas. For example, under the successful Farm & Countryside Initiative, part of the Community Programme, farmers and landowners are being encouraged to generate jobs and training for long-term unemployed people on schemes beneficial to the rural environment and rural communities.

The organisation of MAFF's professional services has also been progressively developed to take account of changing requirements in recent years. In 1971 MAFF's professional, technical and scientific services were brought together in the Agricultural Development & Advisory Service (ADAS). This was organised on a three-tier structure: headquarters to administer policy, regions to deal with co-ordination and management, and divisions to work with local farmers. The new service amalgamated NAAS, the Agricultural Land Service (ALS), the State Veterinary Service and the Drainage and Water Supply Service (DWSS). ADAS gives impartial advice to farmers, growers and landowners, supported by its own laboratories and professional staff. An article by the first Director-General of ADAS in the Ministry's *Bulletin* in 1971 promised that the new service would be smaller, less paternalistic, more cost-conscious and would work on the basis of group advice where possible. In 1980, the ALS and DWSS were merged into a single Land and Water Service (LAWS).

Following UK accession to the European Community, ADAS's role in the transfer of technology became even more important. Great progress has taken place in recent years, and the industry has had to accommodate this while still retaining the old farming skills. ADAS services help farmers with technical expertise, and advice is available on business development, crop, horticulture and livestock management, laboratory and design services. ADAS officers help in the day-to-day running of statutory schemes, for instance, the maintenance of animal health, the Milk & Dairy Regulations, the capital grant schemes and the approval of pesticides.

R & D facilities are provided at the ADAS husbandry farms and horticultural stations, science laboratories and veterinary investigation centres as well as in a number of smaller research units. ADAS runs conferences, on-farm demonstrations, exhibitions and a telephone information service, and issues advisory leaflets and monthly divisional bulletins.

Following an investigation in 1984–5 which identified the industry's view of ADAS and the services it would be prepared to pay for, a range of marketable services was developed in 10 product sectors. A Board of Management was set up and included members drawn from commerce and farming. Services were made available on contract or through special advisory schemes. A basic subscription scheme gives the client telephone access to a wealth of help and information; a premium scheme provides additional hours of consultancy at the client's place of business; group contracts are also available. These services are not only aimed at farmers and growers, but at a much wider range of customers such as agrochemical and other trade organisations, local authorities, landowners and bankers.

In March 1987 the new advisory policy was inaugurated. Although reorganisation of ADAS left the State Veterinary Service unchanged, the remaining services were merged into two new groups: the Farm and Countryside Service

*116. ADAS exhibition stand*

(FCS) and the Research and Development Service (RDS). All the front-line, non-veterinary advice to clients is now provided by the FCS and its new title emphasises the Government's intention to give more weight to the environmental aspects of agricultural advice and to ensure that an adequate balance is maintained between the needs of agriculture, the environment and the rural economy.

The farmer's main task is still to provide food. Consumer tastes and habits are changing. Within a fairly static total population there have been substantial increases in the proportions of old people and of very small households. Social changes, like the rise in the number of working wives, the development of television and the video, the growing practices of eating outside and drinking inside the home, have influenced shopping patterns. Technological changes, including the increased ownership of refrigerators, freezers and the microwave oven, have permitted the development of a much greater range of products and cooking practices. And people are becoming much more aware of the effects of diet on health. These developments have resulted in changes in production, manufacturing and distribution and have resulted in the development of Ministry functions in relation to organic farming, to marketing and to food safety.

# FOOD

The Ministry sponsors the food and drink manufacturing and distribution industries and non-residential catering in the United Kingdom. In the 1970s, the Ministry played an active part in the regulation of pay and prices and in the industrial policy which was then developed. More recently, its principal concerns have been with deregulation in those areas, the protection of food safety, the effects of the Common Agricultural Policy on the supplies and prices of materials for the sponsored industries, exports of food and drink, competition policy and international commodity policy.

The Ministry commissions or itself undertakes a substantial programme of research and development concerned with the improvement of the safety and quality of food and the efficiency of food processing. The commissioned work is carried out by research institutes, the food research associations and the universities.

Farmers and food manufacturers are becoming increasingly interdependent, and the Government encourages the development of agricultural and horticultural co-operation in the UK, mainly through grant schemes administered by the 'Food from Britain' organisation. 'Food from Britain' was launched in March 1983 with the aim of encouraging sales of British food at home and abroad. It took over the work of the now defunct Central Council for Agricultural and Horticultural Co-operation and £14 million was made available by Government over a five-year period to support the promotion and improvement of food and drink marketing. To qualify to use the British food quality mark, products must meet rigorous grading, production, and packaging standards, and be of consistently high quality. Random checks at retail outlets monitor standards, and there are quality schemes for a wide range of products. 'Food from Britain', said the Minister, Peter Walker, at its inception, 'is potentially the most significant development in the farming and food industries this decade'.

There are many exciting developments in food processing and manufacturing. There is a growing understanding of the chemistry and structure of food and of their effects on taste, smell, appearance and texture. This is giving manufacturers greater freedom in the use of raw materials and in the techniques of processing and packaging, permitting lower prices and a wider range of products, meeting consumer needs on such aspects as health and convenience. Novel foods like mycoprotein (a fungus grown in filament form and sold in its own right, not as a meat substitute) are beginning to be developed. There are many developments in the bio-technological field and genetic engineering is promising to provide major new opportunities in the form, for example, of higher yield or greater disease resistance.

So far as consumer protection is concerned, in the course of the 1970s and the 1980s, the Ministry has tended to move away from imposing compositional standards on food. As consumer requirements change and become more complex, these standards gradually become outdated and inhibit the development of new products designed to meet consumer needs. For example, minimum fat content standards at one time prevented the development of low-fat products. Instead, the aim has been to provide more effective ingredient and nutritional labelling so that consumers can decide for themselves what they want to purchase.

A more specific approach is being adopted towards the safety and approval of additives and contaminants. For

*117. Food from Britain
information stand at ISM fair,
Cologne, 1986*

example, colours and flavourings are being considered in detail and legislation has been introduced to prohibit added colourings in food for babies and young children.

A UK National Nutrient Data Bank is to be produced jointly with the Royal Society of Chemistry to help dietary planning and research into the 1990s. This project will update and expand the 1978 edition of McCance and Widdowson's standard work on the composition of foods. Coverage will include more detail on nutrients and newer foods such as low-fat milks and other dairy products. It will also include information on regional differences in nutrient content in selected foods.

MAFF's *Manual of Nutrition* has gone into several editions and is an HMSO best seller. The book describes all the important nutrients, their roles in the body, the foods that provide them and ways in which these foods are digested. It indicates the effects of cooking and processing on each food, shows how to establish sensible eating habits and advises on the different nutritional needs of particular groups of people.

Work continues on reviewing food legislation; proposals have been made and responses received on revision of the Food Acts. Detailed consultation is taking place on such matters as enforcement at factory level, tightening of controls over contaminated or unfit foods (including imports) and over the opening of new food businesses, and

119

control over the development of novel foods and other technological changes.

As food technology advances, the opportunities for improving the quality of supplies and broadening the variety of healthy foods for consumers increases. One example is the proposed use of food irradiation which can reduce the risk of food-borne illnesses, inhibit sprouting of vegetables, delay the ripening of fruit and extend the shelf life of foods. The Advisory Committee on Irradiated and Novel Foods concluded in a report published in 1986 that the irradiation of food up to an overall dose of 10kGy presented no toxicological hazard and introduced no special nutritional problems to the treated foods. The report also recommended that, if irradiation was permitted, irradiated foods should be clearly marked throughout manufacture and at the point of sale. Work is proceeding on the possibilities for permitting use of this technique in the processing of particular groups of products.

The EC dimension in much of this work is important and growing. Regulations made as the result of EC agreements negotiated in Brussels control labelling and various aspects of the composition of various foods, including some sugar products, cocoa and chocolate, coffee, honey, fruit juices, nectars and jams. Others cover additives, colourings, emulsifiers and stabilisers. The Community is working towards the control of all additives used in food throughout Europe by 1992 as part of the programme to complete the EC internal market by then. The aim is to remove non-tariff barriers and establish common rules to create an unrestricted economic area and a genuinely free market for the exchange of goods and services.

MAFF's arrangements to protect the public from contaminated foodstuffs were thoroughly tested by the accident at the Russian nuclear power plant at Chernobyl in April 1986. As soon as elevated levels of radioactivity were detected in Europe and before the radioactive plume actually reached British shores, MAFF began checking for radioactivity and started sampling milk from various areas of England. Once the plume reached the country, radioactivity was rapidly detected in the areas affected by heavy rainfall. The Ministry set up an emergency operations room to manage the situation; this included answering questions from the public (up to 1,000 telephone calls a day). A programme of monitoring all agricultural products was initiated. As a result, it was observed that levels of radioactivity in lamb in certain parts of the country were rising. In June, when there were indications that they would begin to reach unacceptable levels, an emergency Order was made under the Food & Environmental Protection Act 1985, restricting the movement and slaughter of sheep in Cumbria. The other agricultural departments made similar Orders for areas in Wales and Scotland. MAFF's controls remain in force, although the restricted area has been greatly reduced. Sheep in the area have to pass a live-monitoring test before they can be sent to slaughter and compensation is paid to farmers whose flocks are affected. Tests have been and continue to be carried out on agricultural products taken from the restricted area and elsewhere in the country in order to monitor the position and to continue to protect the public from potentially harmful foodstuffs.

# FISHERIES

As with agriculture and food, the work of the MAFF Fisheries Department has evolved to meet the changing economic circumstances of the industry and the need to adapt to EC policies.

European fishermen have faced a difficult period of adjustment over the last two decades. The decline of some important sectors of the industry was due to such factors as lost access to distant fishing grounds, decline in fish stocks because of overfishing, and increases in overhead costs. There are, however, now signs of returning prosperity and confidence.

These changes have taken place alongside the development of a Common Fisheries Policy as envisaged by the Treaty of Rome in 1957, although a long gestation period was required before 'Blue Europe' was born. The first steps were taken in 1970, before the UK joined the European Community, when a common market organisation for fish was created. It aimed to ensure a fair standard of living for those in the industry, to stabilise markets and to guarantee supplies to consumers at reasonable prices. The market organisation provided for the establishment of common marketing standards of size and freshness for fish, together with a price structure for the most important species. The market price support system involved encouraging the formation of voluntary fish producer organisations through which financial compensation was channelled when fish was withdrawn from the market after failing to reach pre-determined Community price levels. The policy also included limited measures to protect the Community market against low-priced imports from third countries.

This policy was then overtaken by the accession of the UK, the Irish Republic and Denmark to the Community

*118. Lowestoft Docks*

and by the general extension of fishery limits to 200 miles. The negotiations for entry themselves profoundly modified the Common Fisheries Policy. There followed a long period of negotiation in which the Ministry played a leading part. It was not until 1983 that agreement was reached on a revised Common Fisheries Policy (CFP) which provides the basis for Community fishing until the year 2002. It established a system for the conservation and management of fish stocks in that part of the EC fishing zone in the North-East Atlantic area. Member states were allowed to retain limits of up to six miles from their own shores for national fleets and a further six miles for national fleets and those with traditional fishing rights. In a larger area around the Orkneys and Shetlands, fishing for potentially endangered species was made subject to a licensing system that limited fishing to a set number of British, French, German and Belgian vessels. The main Atlantic fish stocks were conserved by fixing Total Allowable Catches, to be agreed annually by the Council of Ministers, and divided between the member states on the basis of a fixed key. Other measures to conserve stocks included minimum mesh size for nets and minimum sizes for fish landed.

In addition to these market support measures, grants were provided for the decommissioning, construction and modernisation of vessels, for aquaculture projects, and for construction of artificial reefs to help re-stock inshore waters. Financial help was also made available for measures to create fishing activity in new grounds, to exploit fishery resources in other countries through joint ventures, or to search for under-exploited species. The cost of the CFP is small when compared with its big brother, the CAP. The 1988 Community budget provided for only £28 million to be spent on it (about 0.7% of total Community spending).

Enforcement of all EC fisheries legislation is undertaken by national authorities and monitored by the Commission's Inspectorate. MAFF is responsible for the extensive waters within the UK fishery limits off England and Wales and employs a coordinated enforcement surveillance policy. This integrated service under the operational direction of the Sea Fisheries Inspectorate utilises dedicated ships of the Royal Navy's Fishery Protection Squadron and three purpose-built aircraft operated under civilian contract terms by a company based at Bournemouth.

*119. Fisheries patrol aircraft*

MAFF's Fisheries Department today has a wide range of responsibilities concentrated mainly on the conservation and exploitation of fish stocks in marine and inland waters and the protection of the marine environment. The policy is also concerned with the development of a viable fish farming industry. The Fisheries Department administers the EC Common Fisheries Policy in the UK, and the policy is a major factor in the conservation of the fish stocks in the seas around the UK. The majority of the most important decisions in this area are Community decisions. MAFF, together with the other UK Fisheries Departments, seeks to ensure that the fishing opportunities available to the UK under the CFP are shared out on a fair and reasonable basis among the fishermen concerned. The Directorate of Fisheries Research makes a major input into the stock assessment work which underpins the Community as well as UK national decisions on fish conservation, and the Sea Fisheries Inspectorate is responsible for ensuring that EC and national fishing regulations are respected within UK fishing limits off England and Wales. The Inspectorate also enforces the EC fish grading regulations.

The protection of the aquatic environment involves the headquarter divisions, the Laboratories and the Inspectorate. There is also an important international dimension.

120. Strandline monitoring for
Beta-radioactivity hotspots

The Ministry is a licensing authority in respect of the disposal of waste in the marine environment. The Laboratories are responsible for statutory inspections and aquatic environmental research in connection with the control and disposal of both radioactive and non-radioactive wastes, and the Inspectorate ensures that the necessary regulations and licence conditions are complied with.

Work in relation to the development of the fishing industry includes the provision of grants for the modernisation of harbours, the administration of the EC fish marketing regulations and policies to control fish diseases. The Department works closely with the Sea Fish Industry Authority (which administers the grants for fishing vessels) and the Sea Fisheries Committees and Water Authorities which have responsibilities for regulating coastal and inland fisheries. In 1987 the Government announced plans to transfer the fisheries functions of the Water Authorities to a National Rivers Authority when water supply and sewage disposal activities are due to be privatised.

In all its tasks, the Fisheries Department aims to work in close consultation with the fishing and other interests concerned. Its fundamental objectives are to ensure the long-term conservation of fish stocks and the aquatic environment in the interests of fishermen and the community at large.

# INFORMATION TODAY

The role of MAFF's Information Division is to ensure that the Ministry's policies and services are publicised, promoted and understood – by the industry, the general public and the international community. The Division consists of three branches: Press, Publicity and Libraries.

Press branch advises Ministers and senior officials on everything that involves the media (the national and regional press; radio and television; agencies; specialist journals; overseas correspondents). The branch prepares press notices and features on all aspects of the Ministry's work. It arranges ministerial press conferences, special briefings, photocalls and broadcasting interviews. Press officers accompany ministers on visits throughout the UK and abroad, including regular trips to Brussels and Luxembourg for meetings of the Agriculture and Fisheries Councils. The branch also operates a press cuttings service to keep ministers and officials abreast of what newspapers are saying about the Department and developments within the industries. Television and radio broadcasts are monitored as necessary. Regional information officers based in MAFF's five regions assist Press branch with its work.

Publicity branch is responsible for the 'paid' side of the Division's work. It uses advertising, exhibitions, audiovisual aids, publications and other promotional material to publicise the Department's campaigns. These cover such things as rabies, sheep scab, stubble burning and food additives. The Department has stands at many of the major exhibitions such as the Royal and Smithfield Shows, and also takes part in numerous smaller events. Although the branch has a number of specialists on its staff, such as graphic designers and print procurement experts, it also buys in a lot of its material or services – either directly or through the Central Office of Information.

The Main Library in Whitehall Place has the standing of a national reference library for agriculture and is the centre of a network of 17 major libraries and over 100 library service points throughout the Ministry. Besides the Main Library, there are libraries specialising in food and nutrition, law, economics and computer science. There is a library at each MAFF regional office and a network of other libraries within each region. Specialised libraries serve the laboratories at Harpenden, Slough, Weybridge, Tolworth, Lowestoft, Burnham and Torry.

# CONCLUSION

The Ministry requires a very wide range of expertise to carry out its varied functions. Today MAFF staff numbers are substantially below the peak of 15,000 in the 1960s and early 1970s. The largest group are scientific, professional and technical specialists. Some 70% of the Ministry staff are located in the regions, mainly in five regional and 19 divisional offices. Management of the regional organisation is unified under five regional directors. The State Veterinary Service remains under the central management of the Chief Veterinary Officer and provides services in England, Scotland and Wales. ADAS services are provided to the Secretary of State for Wales on an agency basis. MAFF administers Government policy for agriculture, horticulture and fisheries in England and for food and drink matters in the UK as a whole.

Over the past 100 years, the Ministry has sought to encourage and help the agriculture, fisheries and food industries to meet the needs of UK and overseas consumers in an efficient, safe and humane way. In doing so, it has adapted to widely changing circumstances and governments. It played a crucial role in two world wars. It has been at the heart of the UK's developing membership of the European Community. It is now poised to enter its second century with the recognition that major new challenges lie ahead.

# APPENDICES

# APPENDIX A: MINISTERS AND PERMANENT SECRETARIES

MINISTERS AND PERMANENT SECRETARIES OF THE BOARD OF AGRICULTURE (1889–1903),
THE BOARD OF AGRICULTURE & FISHERIES (1903–1919),
THE MINISTRY OF AGRICULTURE & FISHERIES (1919–1955), THE MINISTRY OF FOOD (1939–1955)
AND THE MINISTRY OF AGRICULTURE, FISHERIES & FOOD

PRESIDENTS OF THE BOARD OF
AGRICULTURE, AND THE BOARD OF
AGRICULTURE & FISHERIES,
MINISTERS OF AGRICULTURE & FISHERIES

*Earl Carrington, President of the
Board of Agriculture and
Fisheries, December 1905–
October 1911*

Rt Hon Henry Chaplin (later Viscount Chaplin), September
1889–August 1892

Rt Hon Herbert Gardner (later Lord Burghclere), August
1892–July 1895

Rt Hon Walter Long (later Viscount Long), July 1895–November
1900

Rt Hon R W Hanbury, November 1900–May 1903

Rt Hon the Earl of Onslow, May 1903–February 1905

Sir Ailwyn Fellowes (later Lord Ailwyn), March 1905–October
1905

Earl Carrington (later Marquis of Lincolnshire), December
1905–October 1911

Rt Hon Walter Runciman (later Viscount Runciman), October
1911–August 1914

Lord Lucas & Dingwall, August 1914–May 1915

Earl of Selborne, May 1915–June 1916

Earl of Crawford & Balcarres, July 1916–December 1916

Lord Ernle (R E Prothero), December 1916–July 1919

Lord Lee of Fareham, January 1920–February 1921

Sir Arthur Griffith Boscawen, February 1921–October 1922

Sir Robert Sanders, October 1922–January 1924

Rt Hon Noel Buxton (later Lord Noel-Buxton), January 1924–
November 1924

Rt Hon Edward Wood (later Lord Irwin), November 1924–
November 1925

Rt Hon Walter Guinness (later Lord Moyne), November
1925–June 1929

Rt Hon Noel Buxton (later Lord Noel-Buxton), June 1929–June
1930

*Tom Williams, Minister of Agriculture and Fisheries, August 1945–October 1951*

Rt Hon Dr Christopher Addison (later Lord Addison), June 1930–August 1931

Sir John Gilmour, August 1931– September 1932

Rt Hon Walter Elliott, October 1932–November 1936

Rt Hon W S Morrison (later Lord Dunrossil), November 1936–February 1939

Sir Reginald Dorman-Smith, February 1939–May 1940

Rt Hon R S Hudson (later Lord Hudson), May 1940–August 1945

Rt Hon Tom Williams (later Lord Williams), August 1945–October 1951

Sir Thomas Dugdale (later Lord Crathorne), November 1951–July 1954

Rt Hon Derick Heathcoat Amory (later Lord Amory), July 1954–January 1958

*Viscount Woolton, Minister of Food, April 1940–November 1943*

*Sir Ben Smith, Minister of Food, August 1945–May 1946*

Rt Hon W S Morrison (later Lord Dunrossil), September 1939–April 1940

Rt Hon Viscount Woolton, April 1940–November 1943

Colonel the Rt Hon J J Llewellin (later Lord Llewellin), November 1943–August 1945

Sir Ben Smith, August 1945–May 1946

Rt Hon John Strachey, May 1946–March 1950

Rt Hon Maurice Webb, March 1950–October 1951

Major the Rt Hon Gwilym Lloyd-George (later Lord Tenby), October 1951–October 1954

Rt Hon Derick Heathcoat Amory (later Lord Amory), October 1954–January 1958 (Combined the separate posts of Minister of Agriculture & Fisheries and Minister of Food, pending the merger of 1955)

## MINISTERS OF AGRICULTURE, FISHERIES & FOOD

*Michael Jopling, Minister of Agriculture, Fisheries and Food, June 1983–June 1987*

Rt Hon Derick Heathcoat Amory (later Lord Amory), 1955–January 1958

Rt Hon John Hare (later Viscount Blakenham), January 1958–July 1960

Rt Hon Christopher Soames (later Lord Soames), July 1960–October 1964

Rt Hon T F Peart (later Lord Peart), October 1964–April 1968

Rt Hon Cledwyn Hughes (later Lord Cledwyn), April 1968–June 1970

Rt Hon James Prior (later Lord Prior), June 1970–November 1972

Rt Hon J B Godber (later Lord Godber), November 1972–March 1974

Rt Hon T F Peart (later Lord Peart), March 1974–September 1976

Rt Hon John Silkin, September 1976–May 1979

Rt Hon Peter Walker, May 1979–June 1983

Rt Hon Michael Jopling, June 1983–June 1987

Rt Hon John MacGregor, June 1987–

## PERMANENT SECRETARIES TO THE BOARD AND MINISTRY OF AGRICULTURE, AND MAFF

*Sir Sydney Olivier, Permanent Secretary to the Board, February 1913–June 1917*

*Sir Daniel Hall, Permanent Secretary to the Board, June 1917–February 1920*

Sir George Leach, September 1889–December 1891

Sir Thomas Elliott, January 1892–February 1913

Sir Sydney Olivier (later Lord Olivier), February 1913–June 1917

Sir Daniel Hall, June 1917–February 1920

*Sir Alan Hitchman, Permanent
Secretary to MAF, October
1952–March 1959*

Sir Francis Floud, March 1920–July 1927
Sir Charles Howell Thomas, August 1927–August 1936
Sir Donald Fergusson, September 1936–May 1945
Sir Donald Vanderpeer, June 1945–September 1952
Sir Alan Hitchman, October 1952–March 1959
Sir John Winnifrith, April 1959–December 1967
Sir Basil Engholm, January 1968–December 1972
Sir Alan Neale, January 1973–December 1978
Sir Frederick Kearns (appointed 2nd Permanent Secretary),
    September 1973–October 1978
Sir Brian Hayes, January 1979–May 1983
Sir Michael Franklin, May 1983–September 1987
Derek Andrews, October 1987–

PERMANENT SECRETARIES TO THE MINISTRY
OF FOOD

*Sir Percival Liesching,
Permanent Secretary to the
Ministry of Food, July 1946–
December 1948*

Sir Henry French, December 1939–December 1945
Sir Frank Tribe, January 1946–July 1946
Sir Percival Liesching, July 1946–December 1948
Sir Frank Lee, January 1949–August 1951
Sir Henry Hancock, August 1951–April 1955

# APPENDIX B: BIBLIOGRAPHY

This bibliography is a list of sources consulted and is not intended as a comprehensive set of references to the Ministry.

## BOOKS AND ARTICLES ON THE BOARD/MINISTRY OF AGRICULTURE, FISHERIES AND FOOD

BOARD OF AGRICULTURE & FISHERIES. Fisheries Division. *British fisheries: reconstruction.* Memorandum prepared by the Board, 1919.

COLLER, Frank. *A state trading adventure.* OUP, 1925.

FLOUD, Sir Francis L C. *The Ministry of Agriculture and Fisheries.* G P Putnam's Sons Ltd, 1927.

JONES, *Sir* Thomas G. *The unbroken front: Ministry of Food, 1916–1944. Personalities and problems.* Everybody's Books, 1944.

*Know your ministry: a description of government departments whose operations affect the conduct of business,* revised and reprinted from the *Midland Bank Review.* Europa Publications Ltd, 1959.

LANCUM, F H. *Press officer please!* Crosby Lockwood & Son Ltd, 1946.

LEE, A J. *A history of fisheries research in MAFF.* (DFR internal report), 1989.

MAFF/DAFS. *A century of agricultural statistics: Great Britain 1866–1966.* HMSO, 1968.

MAFF, Northern Ireland Office, Scottish Office, Welsh Office. *Farming UK.* HMSO, 1987.

MAF. *Fisheries in the Great War, being the report on sea fisheries for the years 1915, 1916, 1917 and 1918 of the Board of Agriculture and Fisheries – parts I and II.* HMSO, 1920 Cmd 585.

MAF. *Fisheries in war time. Report on the sea fisheries of England and Wales for the years 1939–1944 inclusive.* HMSO, 1946.

MAFF. Directorate of Fisheries Research. *Fisheries research: a brief description of the work being done in the Ministry's fisheries laboratories.* Lowestoft, DFR, 1982.

MAFF. *Food additives: the balanced approach.* 1987.

MAFF. *Food quality and safety: a century of progress. Proceedings of the symposium celebrating the centenary of the Sale of Food and Drugs Act 1875.* HMSO, 1976.

MAFF. *Report of the Committee appointed to review the provincial and local organisations and procedures of the Ministry of Agriculture, Fisheries and Food.* HMSO, 1956. Cmd 9732 (Chairman: Sir Arton Wilson).

MINISTRY OF FOOD. *ABC of food rationing in the United Kingdom.* 1951 edition.

MINISTRY OF FOOD. *How Britain was fed in wartime: food control 1939–1945.* HMSO, 1946.

MINISTRY OF FOOD. *Lectures on the administration of food control, rationing and distribution, arranged at the request of the British Council and given at the Carlton Hotel, Haymarket, London W1, 22nd May to 2nd June 1944.* [Typescript]

WINNIFRITH, *Sir* John. *The Ministry of Agriculture, Fisheries and Food.* George Allen & Unwin, 1962.

WISE, E F. 'The history of the Ministry of Food', *Economic Journal, XXXIX,* Dec 1929, pp 566–571.

## GENERAL BOOKS AND ARTICLES

ADDISON, Viscount. *How the Labour Party has saved agriculture: the story of six great years.* Labour Party [1951?].

ADDISON, Paul. *Now the war is over: a social history of Britain 1945–51.* BBC/Cape, 1985.

ALLEN, W Gore. *The reluctant politician: Derick Heathcoat Amory.* Christopher Johnson, 1958.

BARNETT, Margaret. *British food policy during the First World War.* Allen & Unwin, 1985.

BEVERIDGE, William. *British food control.* New York. Carnegie Endowment for International Peace, 1928.

BROCKWAY, T P. *Rationing in Britain, 1939–1945.* 1950 [Preliminary draft of the third volume of a series of studies of rationing during World War Two, undertaken by Harvard University . . .]

BROOKING, Thomas W H. *Agrarian businessmen organise: a comparative study of the origins and early phase of development of the National Farmers' Union of England & Wales and the New Zealand Farmers' Union, ca 1880–1929.* Dissertation submitted for the degree of Doctor of Philosophy, Dept History, University of Otago, Dunedin, New Zealand, Dec 1977.

BROWN, Jonathan. *Agriculture in England: a survey of farming, 1870–1947.* Manchester University Press, 1987.

BRUCE, P J *ed. The kitchen front: 122 recommended recipes selected from broadcasts by Mabel Constanduros, Freddie Grisewood, etc.* Nicholson & Watson, 1942.

BULLETT, Gerald. *Achievement in feeding Britain.* The Pilot Press Ltd [1944] (Achievement books No. 5.)

BURK, K *ed. War and the state: the transformation of British government 1914–1919.* Allen & Unwin, 1982.

BURK, Marguerite C. 'The National Food Survey of the United Kingdom and comparisons with other British and American food data'. *Agricultural Economics Research IX* (3) July 1957. 15pp.

BURNETT, J. *Plenty and want: a social history of diet in England from 1815 to the present day*. Nelson, 1966, Pelican Books, 1968.

BUTTON, Henry. 'One hundred and fifty years ago: agriculture in the time of the Prince Regent'. *Agriculture 76* 1969, pp 439–444.

CALDER, Angus. *The people's war: Britain 1939–45*. Cape, 1969, Granada, 1971, reprinted 1982.

CENTRAL OFFICE OF INFORMATION. *Agriculture in Britain*. COI, 1985 (Ref pamphlet no 1, no 55/85).

CENTRAL OFFICE OF INFORMATION. Reference division. Home front section. *Rationing and distribution schemes in Great Britain*. COI, 1944.

'The Central Veterinary Laboratory Weybridge, 1917–1967: a record of its origin, its fifty years of development and its contribution to veterinary research'. *The Veterinary Record 15* July 1967, pp 62–68.

CHAMBERS, J D. *Laxton: the last English open field village*. HMSO, 1964.

CLARKE, Ernest. 'The Board of Agriculture 1793–1822' *Journal of the Royal Agricultural Society of England IX*, 1898, pp 1–41.

CLYNES, J R. 'Food control in war and peace'. *Economic Journal XXX*, June 1920, pp 147–155.

CRAFTER, F & REDMAN, N, *compilers. A short history of 20 years: The Agricultural Training Board 1966–1986*. 1986.

CRAIG, *Sir* J. *A history of red tape: an account of the origin and development of the civil service*. Macdonald & Evans Ltd, 1955.

DAKERS, Caroline. *The countryside at war 1914–1918*. Constable, 1987.

D'ENNO, Douglas. 'When hard times were on the cards'. *Bulletin of the Ministry of Agriculture, Fisheries and Food*, July and August 1982.

DIACK, William. 'British farmers and the war' *Contemporary Review*, April 1915, pp 479–486.

EASTERBROOK, L F *ed. The future of agriculture*. Todd Publishing Co, 1944.

ERNLE, *Lord. Whippingham to Westminster: the reminiscences of Lord Ernle (Rowland Prothero)*. John Murray, 1938.

*Final Act of the United Nations Conference on Food and Agriculture*. Hot Springs, Virginia, USA, 18th May–3rd June, 1943. HMSO, 1943, Cmd 6451.

FLETCHER, T W. 'British agriculture 1894–2000' *Agriculture 76*, September 1969, pp 464–467.

FOOD (WAR) COMMITTEE. *Report on the food supply of the UK*. HMSO, 1917, Cd 8421.

FUSSELL, G E. 'The collection of agricultural statistics in Great Britain: its origin and evolution'. *Agricultural History 18* (4) October 1944, pp 161–167.

GILCHRIST, *Sir* Andrew. *Cod Wars and how to lose them*. Edinburgh. Q Press, 1978.

GOODWIN, F H. 'The rights of a plant breeder'. *Scientific Horticulture 35*, 1984, pp 88–93.

GRAHAM, Michael. *The fish gate*. Faber & Faber, 1943.

GRIMSDALE, Peter. 'When food was short'. *Caterer & Hotelkeeper 176* (3388) 26 September 1985, pp 89, 91.

HAMMOND, R J. *Food and agriculture in Britain 1939–1945: aspects of wartime control*. Stanford University Press, 1954.

HARMAN, Tony. *Seventy summers: the story of a farm*. BBC Publications, 1986.

HAY, Roy. *Gardener's chance: from war production to peace possibilities*. Putnam & Co Ltd, 1946.

HEPPER, F N, *ed. Royal Botanic Gardens Kew: gardens for science and pleasure*. HMSO, 1982.

HESS, Lou. 'Lending a hand on the land 1939–1945'. *MAFF Bulletin* May 1983, pp 18–20.

HILL, *Lord*, of Luton. *Both sides of the hill*. Heinemann, 1964.

HOLDERNESS, B A. *British agriculture since 1945*. Manchester University Press, 1985.

'Impresario'. *The market square: the story of the Food Ration Book 1940–1944*. 1944.

INTERNATIONAL LABOUR OFFICE. *Food control in Great Britain*. Montreal. International Labour Office, 1943 (Studies and reports, series B (Economic conditions) no 35).

JENKINS, J T. *The sea fisheries*. Constable, 1920.

JUKES, D J. *Food legislation of the UK: a concise guide*. Butterworths, 1984.

KINLOCH, Ian. *Don't forget your wellies*. Providence Press, 1983.

*The Land Girl*, April 1940–March 1942.

*The Landswoman*, January 1918–December 1920.

LEWIS, Peter. *A people's war*. Thames Methuen, 1986.

THE LIBRARY, University of Reading. *Historical farm records: a summary guide to manuscripts and other material in the University Library*, collected by the Institute of Agricultural History and the Museum of English Rural Life, compiled by J Edwards, 1973.

LONGMATE, Norman, *ed. The home front: an anthology of personal experience 1938–1945*. Chatto & Windus, 1981.

LONGMATE, Norman. *How we lived then: a history of everyday life during the Second World War*. Arrow Books, 1973.

LOOSMORE, R M. 'The veterinary investigation service in England & Wales'. *The Veterinarian I*, 1963, pp 19–27.

MACQUEEN, M. 'The training of women on the land'. *Journal of the Board of Agriculture XXV* (7) October 1918, pp 810–817.

MARSHALL, Janette. 'When Britain ate for health'. *Here's Health*, April 1983, pp 16–22.

MARWICK, A. *Women at war 1914–1918.* Croom Helm, 1977.

MIDDLETON, T H M. *Food production in war.* OUP, 1923.

MINISTRY OF INFORMATION. *Land at war: the official story of British farming 1939–1944.* HMSO, 1945.

MINNS, Raynes. *Bombers and mash: the domestic front 1939–45.* Virago, 1980.

MURRAY, K A H. *Agriculture.* HMSO/Longmans Green & Co, 1955 (Civil history of the second world war).

NAPOLITAN, L. 'The centenary of the agricultural census'. *Journal of the Royal Agricultural Society of England 127*, 1966, pp 81–86.

O'HANLON, S R. 'Who serve the land' *Agriculture 76*, 1969, pp 468–471.

ORWIN, C S & WHETHAM, E H. *History of British agriculture 1846–1914.* Longmans, 1964.

PARSONS, L M. 'Land Commissioners of England 1894'. *Agriculture 76*, 1969, pp 454–459.

PEARCE, J W R and others. *Animal health: a centenary 1865–1965. A century of endeavour to control diseases of animals.* HMSO, 1965.

PLIMMER, V G. *Food values in wartime.* Longmans Green & Co, 1941.

POSTLETHWAITE, J R P. *I look back.* T V Boardman & Co Ltd, 1947.

PUBLIC RECORD OFFICE. *The second world war: a guide to documents in the Public Record Office.* HMSO, 1972.

[WRIGHT, Harold]. *Letters of Stephen Reynolds.* Hogarth Press, 1923.

ROYAL INSTITUTE OF PUBLIC ADMINISTRATION. *The organisation of British central government 1914–1964: a survey by a study group of the . . . Institute*, edited by D N Chester, written by F M G Willson. 2nd ed. Allen & Unwin, 1968.

SACKVILLE-WEST, Vita. *The women's land army.* Michael Joseph Ltd, 1944.

SEYMOUR, W ed. *A history of the Ordnance Survey.* Wm Dawson & Sons, 1980.

SHELTON, Jim. 'Fifty years of food control?' *Chemistry & Industry*, 20 March 1972, pp 193–196.

SHERWELL-COOPER, W E. *Land girl: a manual for volunteers in the women's land army.* English Universities Press, 1941.

SISSONS, M & French, P eds. *Age of austerity 1945–51.* Hodder & Stoughton, 1963, Penguin Books, 1964.

STETTINIUS, Edward R Jr. *Lend-lease: weapon for victory.* Macmillan, 1944.

TALBOT, Meriel L. 'Women in agriculture during wartime'. *Journal of the Board of Agriculture XXV* (7) October 1918, pp 796–805.

TURNER, Alan. 'The development and structure of food legislation in the United Kingdom and its interaction with European Community food laws'. *Food Drug Cosmetic Law Journal 39*, 1984, pp 430–444.

VERNON, R V & MANSERGH, N eds. *Advisory bodies: a study of their uses in relation to central government 1919–1939.* Allen & Unwin, 1940.

WATERMAN, J J. *Torry Research Station 1929–1979: a brief history.* [1979]

WHITLOCK, Ralph. *The great cattle plague: an account of the foot-and-mouth epidemic of 1967–8.* John Baker, 1968.

LORD WILLIAMS OF BARNBURGH. *Digging for Britain.* Hutchinson, 1965.

WOOD, Walter. *Fishermen in wartime.* Sampson Low, Marston & Co, [1918].

*The memoirs of the Rt Hon the Earl of Woolton.* Cassell, 1959.

YASS, Marion. *This is your war: home front propaganda in the second world war.* Public Record Office, HMSO, 1983.

134

# APPENDIX C: CHRONOLOGY

1793 Board or Society for the Encouragement of Agriculture and Internal Improvement founded by Royal Charter.

1833 Agricultural Labourers Union formed at Tolpuddle.

1838 Royal Agricultural Society of England founded (incorporated by Royal Charter in 1840).

1841 Tithe Commission set up under Tithe Act 1836.

1846 First Land Drainage Act authorised issue of loans from public funds to enable landowners to carry out drainage works.

1860 Adulteration of Food & Drink Act passed. First general pure food law to be published in any English-speaking country.

1865 Cattle Plague Department set up as a branch of the Home Office to deal with outbreak of rinderpest.

1866 Cattle Disease Prevention Act ordered slaughter of infected animals, restriction of animal movements and compensation for owners.

Cattle Plague Department transferred to Privy Council.

First annual agricultural census published, comprising livestock returns and crops and grass statistics.

1869 Adulteration of Seeds Act made it an offence to sell any killed or dyed seeds in the UK.

Cattle Plague Department's name changed to Veterinary Department.

1872 National Agricultural Labourers' Union founded.

1875 Sale of Food & Drugs Act made it an offence to sell to the prejudice of the purchaser any article of food or anything not of the nature, substance or quality demanded.

1877 Destructive Insects Act.

1879 Royal Commission on the Depressed Condition of the Agricultural Interest appointed, with Duke of Richmond as chairman.

1882 Settled Land Act amalgamated the Enclosure Commissioners, Copyhold Commissioners and Tithe Commissioners under the title of the Land Commissioners for England and Wales, responsible to the Home Secretary.

1883 Veterinary Department of the Privy Council took over publication of the annual agricultural statistics from the Board of Trade. Renamed Agricultural Department.

1884 Marine Biological Association formed.

1885 Collection of fisheries statistics began.

1889 Board of Agriculture Act passed 12 August, by which Government responsibilities for agricultural matters were combined in one department.

Board of Agriculture established and took over powers and duties of the Lord Commissioners, and those of the Privy Council's Veterinary Department, responsibility for forestry, for collection and preparation of statistics and for agricultural research and education.

Workers' Union set up.

1890 Board of Agriculture took responsibility for Ordnance Survey from the Commissioners of Works & Public Buildings.

1894 Diseases of Animals Act.
*Journal of the Board of Agriculture* first published.

1900 First seed testing station established, in Ireland.

1902 Marine Biological Laboratory opened in Lowestoft.
International Council for the Exploration of the Sea set up.
Rabies eliminated from Britain for first time.

1903 Royal Botanic Gardens, Kew transferred from Commissioners of Works & Public Buildings to Board of Agriculture by Order in Council.

Board of Agriculture became Board of Agriculture and Fisheries and took over certain powers and duties relating to the fishing industry from the Board of Trade.

Imperial Preference Campaign launched by Joseph Chamberlain.

1904 Honorary agricultural correspondents appointed to liaise with Board on regional matters and give advice to farmers.

1906 Eastern Counties Agricultural Labourers and Small Holders Union set up.

1907 Salmon & Freshwater Fisheries Act empowered Board of Agriculture and Fisheries to constitute and regulate fishery boards and districts.

1908 Board of Agriculture takes responsibility for fisheries research.

Board takes over responsibility for allotments.

National Farmers' Union founded.

1909 Royal Commission on Coast Erosion and Afforestation recommends establishment of Forestry Board.

1910 Development Commissioners made responsible for distribution of money for development of agriculture, forestry, harbours and fisheries.

Fisheries Laboratory at Lowestoft closed and staff transferred to Board of Agriculture and moved to London.

1911 Board of Agriculture for Scotland set up and assumed responsibility for all agricultural duties relating to Scotland except in the area of animal health.

1912 Responsibility for farm institutes and other agricultural education financed from Development Fund passed to Board.

1914 War declared, 4 August.
Plant pathology unit established at Kew.
Royal Commission on Sugar Supplies set up.

1915 Agricultural education conference.
Fishery Harbours Act.

1916 Ministry of Food set up under provisions of New Ministries & Secretaries Act and Food Controller, Lord Devonport, appointed.
Rowland Prothero appointed President of the Board of Agriculture and Fisheries.
Wheat Commission set up by Walter Runciman.
National Stud established and placed under control of Board.

1917 Food Production Department set up, first as integral part of Board, then as separate Department responsible to the President of the Board of Agriculture and Fisheries.
Women's branch of the Board of Agriculture and Fisheries established.
Women's Land Army created.
Lord Devonport resigned and Lord Rhondda became Food Controller in June.
*National Food Journal* first published on 12 September.
Corn Production Act guaranteed prices of wheat and oats and a minimum wage to agricultural labourers.
Agricultural Wages Board set up under Corn Production Act.
Central Veterinary Laboratory building at Weybridge opened.
Official seed testing station established in London.
Fisheries Laboratory re-established at Lowestoft.

1918 Death of Lord Rhondda, Food Controller, 3 July.
Armistice day, 11 November.
Women's Land Army disbanded.
Plant Pathology Laboratory set up at Royal Botanic Gardens, Kew.
Fisheries Experiment Station established at Conwy.

1919 Resignation of Food Controller and Permanent Secretary.
Board of Agriculture abolished and reconstituted as Ministry of Agriculture under Ministry of Agriculture & Fisheries Act.

Food Production Department disbanded and work absorbed within Board.
Forestry Act established Forestry Commission.

1920 Agriculture Act laid down new guaranteed price for wheat and oats.
Seeds Act required sellers to disclose essential information on analytical purity and germination to buyers.
Plant Pathology Laboratory moved to Harpenden.

1921 Ministry of Food closed.
Corn Production Acts (Repeal) Act cancelled financial provisions, withdrew guarantees and replaced them with lump sum payments and abolished Agricultural Wages Board.
Department of Agriculture for Northern Ireland set up.
Official seed testing station moved to Cambridge.

1922 Committee on the distribution and prices of agricultural produce appointed under chairmanship of Marquess of Linlithgow.

1922 First veterinary advisory officer appointed (at Cardiff).
National Fruit Trials established at Wisley.

1924 Agricultural Wages (Regulation) Act.
Central Wages Board and Agricultural Wages Committees formed.

1925 Agricultural Returns Act.
Food Council appointed, reporting to Board of Trade.
Public Health (Preservatives etc. in Food) Regulations.

1926 General Strike.

1928 Food & Drugs (Adulteration) Act repealed the 1875 Sale of Food and Drugs act.
Agricultural Produce (Grading & Marking) Act enabled agricultural Ministers to prescribe standard quality grades, packages and methods of packing and to control use of a common trade mark 'The national mark'.
Agricultural Credits Act established the Agricultural Mortgage Corporation which made loans for purchase and improvement of agricultural land.

1929 Torry Research Station founded at Aberdeen.

1930 Land Drainage Act consolidated the law and created Catchment Boards with powers of enforcement for rivers.

1931 Agricultural Marketing Act designed to secure more efficient and economical marketing performance and to improve producers' bargaining power with large-scale processors and distributors. Marketing Boards for hops, milk, bacon and potatoes were set up and exercised control over supply by determination of grade or price.
Agricultural Research Council established by Royal Charter.

1932 Import Duties Act imposed general tariff of 10% on most imports including food. Tariff protection was granted for a wide range of fruit, vegetables and other horticultural produce, and quota restrictions imposed on imports of bacon, ham and other meat products.

Wheat Act under which deficiency payments were made to wheat growers, and the Wheat Commission was set up.

Hops Marketing Scheme in operation.

1933 Agricultural Marketing Act.

Milk marketing scheme in operation, also schemes for pigs and bacon introduced.

Sea Fish Commission appointed under Sir Andrew Duncan to investigate fishing industry.

Consumers' Committees for Great Britain and England & Wales appointed with duty of reporting to Ministers on the progress of the agricultural marketing schemes.

1934 Agricultural radio broadcasts began.

Economic Advisory Committee on Cattle Diseases recommends obligatory routine testing of herds and dairies and expansion of veterinary service.

Land Settlement Association created by Government.

1935 Herring Industry Board established by Herring Industry Act 1935 with powers to develop and regulate the herring industry and grant loans for construction and improvement of boats and equipment.

1936 Sub-committee of Imperial Defence Committee appointed to look into question of food supply during war.

Food (Defence Plans) Department set up within Board of Trade.

Creation of British Sugar Corporation and establishment of Sugar Commission.

Duncan Commission report on white fish industry (Cmd 5130).

Farm Management Survey started.

Tithe Redemption Commission set up under Tithe Act 1936.

1937 Agriculture Act amalgamated all the veterinary services into one national service.

Diseases of Fish Act prohibited import of live salmon and trout and made MAF responsible for dealing with infection in rivers and fish farms.

Livestock Commission established.

1938 White Fish Commission created, but wound up at outbreak of war.

Food & Drugs Act combined food and drug legislation and all the public health legislation relating to food.

Bacon Industry Act established Bacon Development Board.

1939 War declared, 3 September.

Ministry of Food formed, 8 September.

Recruiting began for Women's Land Army.

1940 National Food Survey Committee's annual report on household food consumption and expenditure instituted.

National farm survey began.

Food rationing started.

Lord Woolton became Minister of Food.

Pest Infestation Laboratory set up at Slough by DSIR.

1941 United States Lend-Lease act under which American food, agricultural machinery and equipment was sent to Britain.

MAF's Goods and Services Scheme.

Agricultural Improvement Council for England & Wales founded.

1942 Crop Protection Products Approval Scheme set up.

1943 Hot Springs World Food Conference.

Report of Luxmoore Committee on Agricultural Education (Cmd 6433) recommended that agricultural advisory services should be brought under unified command.

1945 War ended.

Lend-lease suspended.

British Housewives' League founded.

Forestry Commission reconstituted, power of acquiring land for forestry transferred to the Minister for Agriculture & Fisheries.

Food & Agriculture Organization founded.

1946 National Agricultural Advisory Service established.

International Overfishing Conference and Convention prescribes minimum sizes of mesh of nets and minimum size limits of fish caught.

Rationing of bread, cake, flour and oatmeal imposed in July.

National Fruit Trials came under National Agricultural Advisory Service.

Functions relating to agricultural research, advisory and education services transferred from the Development Commission to the agricultural departments.

1947 Agriculture Act passed, with the aim of promoting and maintaining, by provision of guaranteed prices and assured markets, a stable and efficient agricultural industry at minimum prices consistent with proper remuneration and living conditions.

Agricultural Land Service and Agricultural Land Commission set up.

Food Standards Committee founded by Ministry of Food

to advise Ministers on the composition, description, labelling and advertising of food.

General Agreement on Tariffs and Trade (GATT) concluded.

Finance for agricultural departments of universities included in UGC grants.

1948 River Boards Act passed, by which each river system was brought under the control of a single authority.

*NAAS Quarterly Review* first published.

1950 Women's Land Army disbanded.

1952 First Anglo–Icelandic dispute. Icelandic waters closed in May (4-mile fishing limit).

1953 White Fish & Herring Industries Act.

Fisheries Laboratory established at Burnham-on-Crouch.

1954 Posts of Minister of Agriculture & Fisheries and Minister of Food held by one man (Rt Hon Derick Heathcoat Amory) pending merger.

Advisory Committee for Pesticides set up, leading to pesticides safety precaution scheme.

Pre-war Marketing Boards revived.

1955 Ministry of Food amalgamated with MAF and Ministry of Agriculture, Fisheries & Food born, 12 April.

Primary responsibility for food hygiene functions in England & Wales transferred to Ministry of Health.

Lowestoft Fisheries Research Laboratory moved to Grand Hotel site.

Food & Drugs Act sought to ensure that the consumer could buy safe wholesome food and would not be misled as to its character or quality.

1957 Agriculture Act gave long term assurances on prices and extended range of grants for land, building and herd improvements.

BBC started agricultural television service.

Report of the Committee on Horticultural Marketing. (Cmnd 61) (Chairman: Viscount Runciman).

Committee on Transactions in Seeds, first report issued (Cmnd 300).

1958 Wheat Commission dissolved and assets transferred to MAFF.

1959 Kew bicentenary.

Farm institutes and other agricultural education activities of local authorities within remit of Department of Education and Science.

Pest Infestation Laboratory transferred to Agricultural Research Council.

1960 Department of Agriculture for Scotland renamed Department of Agriculture & Fisheries for Scotland (DAFS).

Horticultural Marketing Council set up.

Plant Pathology Laboratory moved to present site.

Committee on Transactions in Seeds issues report recommending Plant Breeders' Rights system of protection (Cmnd 1092).

1961 Covent Garden Market Authority established.

First Cod War settled (fishing limits extended to 12 miles).

1962 Sea Fish Industry Act passed as a result of report of Committee of inquiry into the fishing industry.

Codex Alimentarius Commission founded.

1963 Britain ceased all whaling activities.

National Stud transferred to Horserace Betting Levy Board.

1964 Agricultural & Horticultural Act.

Plant Varieties & Seeds Act.

Agricultural Land Commission and Welsh Agricultural Land sub-Commission dissolved and all rights and liabilities transferred to MAFF.

Food Additives & Contaminants Committee set up.

1965 Ordnance Survey moved to Ministry of Land & Natural Resources.

Wakehurst Place, Sussex acquired by Kew on lease.

Torry transfers from DSIR to MinTech.

Home-Grown Cereals Authority established under Cereal Marketing Act 1965.

1966 Agricultural Training Board established.

1967 Central Council for Agricultural & Horticultural Co-operation established under Agriculture Act 1967 with duty to develop co-operation among producers and to operate grant system for co-operative activities.

Apple & Pear Development Council founded.

Plant Health Act.

Meat & Livestock Commission established under Agriculture Act 1967.

1968 Countryside Act laid down that MAFF should advise those carrying on agricultural businesses on conservation of beauty and amenity of the countryside.

1969 Fish Diseases Laboratory set up at Weymouth.

1970 Pest Infestation Laboratory moved to MAFF and was combined with MAFF's Infestation Control Laboratory.

Common Market organisation for fish created.

Torry transferred to DTI.

1971 Agricultural Development and Advisory Service (ADAS) united MAFF's professional, technical and scientific services.

Veterinary Service incorporated within ADAS.

1972 European Communities Act.

Torry Research Station moves to MAFF and becomes

linked with the fisheries laboratories at Lowestoft and Aberdeen.

Intervention Board for Agricultural Produce set up with responsibility for intervention purchases and sales, payment of export/import refunds, production levies.

1973 UK accedes to European Community.

Water Act changed structure of industry and created 10 water authorities to take on water supply and sewage functions and the functions of former river authorities, including duty to maintain, improve and develop fisheries.

Second Cod War settled (50 mile fishing limit).

1974 MAFF acquired responsibility for protection of marine environment from pollution, under Dumping at Sea Act 1974.

Covent Garden Market moves to new site at Nine Elms.

Drug provisions of Food & Drugs Act 1955 superseded by Medicines Act 1968.

Health & Safety at Work etc. Act.

Pest Infestation Laboratory becomes part of ADAS.

1975 Salmon & Freshwater Fisheries Act.

1976 Land Drainage Act consolidated the law and empowered water authorities to exercise general supervision over land drainage matters.

Agreement reached with Iceland over third Cod War (British trawlers fishing within a 200 mile zone limited to 24 trawlers a day).

1980 Agricultural Land Service and Drainage & Water Supply Service merged into single Land & Water Service (LAWS).

Bees Act.

1981 Wildlife & Countryside Act lays down that MAFF must give advice to those carrying on agricultural businesses on conservation of the countryside and diversification into other enterprises of benefit to the rural economy.

1983 Central Council for Agricultural & Horticultural Co-operation dissolved and work transferred to Food from Britain.

Food from Britain launched, with aim of encouraging growers and manufacturers to make home produced food readily identifiable and to support promotion and improvement of food and drink marketing.

Labelling regulations came into force.

Food Advisory Committee formed out of the Food Standards Committee and the Food Additives & Contaminants Committee.

Common Fisheries Policy agreed.

Diseases of Fish Act enabled MAFF to introduce system of fish registration.

1984 Food Act consolidated the law, its main provisions being to protect the consumer from sale of food considered injurious to health, unfit for human consumption or not of the nature, substance or quality demanded.

Thames Tidal Flood Prevention Scheme opened.

Royal Botanic Gardens, Kew, administered by independent Board of Trustees under provisions of National Heritage Act 1983.

1985 Food & Environment Protection Act passed, covering contamination of food, deposits in the sea, and pesticides.

Land Settlement Association wound up.

New Agriculture Improvement Schemes introduced.

1986 Agriculture Act under which the Minister has a duty to achieve a balance between promotion and maintenance of an efficient and stable agriculture industry, economic and social interests of rural areas, conservation of the natural beauty and amenity of the countryside and promotion of its enjoyment by the public. Also covers designation of Environmentally Sensitive Areas.

Salmon Act created offences of handling illegally caught salmon and provided for establishment of salmon dealer licensing schemes.

Horticultural Development Council set up.

Alternative Lane Use and the Rural Economy (ALURE) working party set up.

Chernobyl accident.

1987 ADAS reorganised and services other than State Veterinary Service merged into Farm & Countryside Service (FCS) and the Research & Development Service (RDS).

*Farming and the rural enterprise* sets out new policies for alternative land use, diversification and the environment.

Princess of Wales Conservatory opened at Kew.

1988 European summit meeting at Rhodes agrees to impose legally binding ceilings on the total agricultural spending and on the annual increases; stabilisers on all major commodities; set-aside scheme for arable crops.

Farm Diversification Grants Scheme introduced.

Environmentally Sensitive Areas, publicity leaflets launched.

Farm Land & Rural Development Act.

Chernobyl: MAFF memorandum to House of Commons Select Committee on Agriculture enquiry.

Farm set-aside scheme launched.

Farm Woodland Scheme introduced.

*Sir George Leach, Permanent Secretary to the Board, September 1889–December 1891*

*Sir Thomas Elliott, Permanent Secretary to the Board, 1892–1913*

*Sir Charles Howell Thomas, Permanent Secretary to the Ministry of Agriculture and Fisheries, 1927–1936*

*Sir Henry French, Permanent Secretary to the Ministry of Food, 1939–1945*

*Sir Donald Vanderpeer,*
*Permanent Secretary to the*
*Ministry of Agriculture and*
*Fisheries, 1945–1952*

*Sir Alan Neale, Permanent*
*Secretary to the Ministry of*
*Agriculture, Fisheries and Food,*
*1973–1978*

*Sir Frank Lee, Permanent*
*Secretary to the Ministry of Food,*
*1949–1951*

*Sir Michael Franklin, Permanent*
*Secretary to the Ministry of*
*Agriculture, Fisheries and Food,*
*1983–1987*

# INDEX

*Numbers in italic refer to pictures; names of publications and ships are also in italic*